THE HOTEL INDUSTRY'S RETENTION MANAGEMENT'S SUCCESS FACTORS OF SELECTED MAJOR HOTELS IN ABU DHABI, UNITED ARAB EMIRATES

Dr. Eileen L. Guerra - Papellero

PARTRIDGE

Copyright © 2019 by Dr. Eileen L. Guerra - Papellero.

Library of Congress Control Number: 2019912229
ISBN: Softcover   978-1-5437-5342-4
               eBook   978-1-5437-5343-1

All rights reserved. No part of this book may be used or reproduced by any means, graphic, electronic, or mechanical, including photocopying, recording, taping or by any information storage retrieval system without the written permission of the author except in the case of brief quotations embodied in critical articles and reviews.

Because of the dynamic nature of the Internet, any web addresses or links contained in this book may have changed since publication and may no longer be valid. The views expressed in this work are solely those of the author and do not necessarily reflect the views of the publisher, and the publisher hereby disclaims any responsibility for them.

Print information available on the last page.

To order additional copies of this book, contact
Toll Free 800 101 2657 (Singapore)
Toll Free 1 800 81 7340 (Malaysia)
orders.singapore@partridgepublishing.com

www.partridgepublishing.com/singapore

DEDICATION

This piece of work is lovingly dedicated to my beloved husband,
our dear children, to my beloved parents, dear parents-in-law,
and to all my loving relatives who in a way or the
other support me in my pursuit for excellence
in business management. Most importantly, all the
glory and honor, always belong to the Almighty God, with
His Son Jesus our Savior, through the power of the Holy Spirit
who reigns forever and ever, AMEN!

EILEEN GUERRA-PAPELLERO

ACKNOWLEDGMENT

I acknowledge the following honorable persons who supported me throughout my journey to becoming a Doctor of Philosophy in Business Management:
To Dr. Eduardo P. Malagapo, my dear professor and esteemed Dean who mentored me starting from my MBA towards the end of my Ph.D. degree in Business Management, that without his continuous monitoring and enthusiastic follow-up this research paper cannot be completed, my academic standing likewise, would come to a halt;
To the members of the defense panel headed by the Chairman, Dr. Junifen Gauuan and his members, Dr. Kathleen Guimbatan, Dr. Alexander Acosta, Dr. Imee Acosta, and Dr. Genaro Japos that with their painstakingly reviewing of my manuscripts and making comments for the good of my study, thus, making it done scholarly.
To my classmates of the EPM & Associates – PCU Graduate School Middle East in all areas where the programs are held monthly, your fantastic help and continuous support especially in our group case studies and group reporting, you made me feel secure in the preparation of our assigned tasks and made it happened by

completing and passing each subject;
To my colleagues in the Hotel Industry
who supported me in filling the
Survey Questionnaire and submitted the data on time, many
thanks for your kindness and goodness;
Special Thanks is accorded to Mr. Joey Cabico and his family
for their encouragement and patience in helping me gather
information vital to the completion of this study and To
Dr. Jose Pascua, for his expert pieces of advice and unselfish
sharing of assessments for the development of the study.
To the Almighty God the Father through His Son Jesus and the
Power of the Holy Spirit, this unique manuscript is
lovingly dedicated to you;

TO GOD BE ALL THE GLORY, HONOR,
AND POWER, FOREVER!

EILEEN GUERRA-PAPELLERO

ABSTRACT

This study aims to assess in the hotel industry's retention management of the rank-and-file employees in terms of the demographic profiles and the level of influence and level of importance of the success factors of selected major hotels operating in Abu Dhabi of the United Arab Emirates as assessed by the managers.

The descriptive-correlational research was applied. The researcher prepared a structured survey questionnaire. It examines the current phenomenon that happens within Abu Dhabi's hotel industry. The eight factors used throughout this study comprises of compensation and benefits, rewards and recognition, work environment and culture, recruitment and selection, career development and training, job design and work teams, performance and management evaluation, and communications.

Correlation analysis tested the relationship between a profile of the respondents and their perceptions on the level of influence and level of importance of the factors of employee retention, and the difference between the perception of managers and rank-and-file employees on the level of importance and level of influence of the success factors of employee retention.

The findings show that the role of the manager in the retention management of the rank-and-file employees was due to the level of influence and level of importance. As to the level of influence, the work environment and corporate culture were assessed by the managers to be the most influential success factor which was followed by performance management and evaluation, and job design and work teams. As to the level of importance, communication was assessed as the most important among all retention factors. The reason is due to good communication skill expected in the hospitality industry. Other considerations was on the recruitment and selection and performance management and evaluation.

As a conclusion, the five success factors that helped the hotel industry in retaining their good employees for sustainable operations, include the work environment and corporate culture, performance management and evaluation, job design and work teams, communication, and recruitment and selection.

As a result of the study, it is recommended that the hotel management should maintain the relationship of the level of influence and the level of importance with the respondents' profiles in terms of age, highest educational attainment, hotel classification, position, and years of service basing from their significance and the rejection of the hypothesis.

Key Terms: Descriptive-Correlational type of Research, Level of Influence, Level of Importance, Success Factors, Retention Management, Hotel Industry in Abu Dhabi.

TABLE OF CONTENTS

Dedication v
Acknowledgment vii
Abstract.. ix

Chapter I   The Problem And Its Background 1

    1. Introduction 1
    2. The Background of the Study 2
    3. Theoretical Framework 3
    4. Conceptual Paradigm 6
    5. Research Objectives 9
    6. Statement of the Problem 10
    7. Statement of Null Hypotheses 11
    8. Significance of the Study 11
    9. Scope and Limitations of the Study 12
    10. Definition of Terms 13

Chapter II   Review Of Related Literature And Studies 15

    1. Local Literature 15
    2. Literature/Studies 25
    3. Retention Management 28
    4. Strategic Human Resource Management 32
    5. Recruitment and Selection 33

    6. Employee Engagement 33
    7. Working Environment and Company Culture.................34
    8. Job Design and Work Team 34
    9. Career Development and Training 35
    10. Performance Management and Evaluation....................36
    11. Communication 39
    12. Other Factors Affecting Employee Retention 41
    13. Compensation and Benefits..42
    14. Recognition and Awards...45
    15. Synthesis of the Study.. 46

Chapter III Research Methodology 50

    1. Research Design...50
    2. Researcher's Sources of Data..51
    3. Sampling Design 51
    4. Research Instrument 52
    5. Data Gathering Procedure...53
    6. Statistical Treatment of Data...55

Chapter IV Results And Discussions..57

    1. The Extent of the Respondents' Demographic Profiles 57
    2. Respondents' Assessment in the Hotel
        Industry's Managers and Rank-and-
        file Employees through the Retention
        Management's Success Factors..62
    3. Significant Relationship between the
        Demographic Profiles of the Respondents
        and the Level of Influence and Level of
        Importance of Retention Factors 80

  4. Significant Differences between the Assessments of the Respondents on the Influence and the Level of Importance of Retention Factors 86
  5. The role of managers in the retention management of rank-and-file employees 89

Chapter V Summary, Conclusion, And Recommendations 93

  1. The Extent of the Respondents' Demographic Profiles 93
  2. Respondents' Assessment in the Hotel Industry's Rank-and-file Employees through the Retention Management's Success Factors 95
  3. Significant Relationship between the Demographic Profiles of the Respondents and the Influence and the Level of Importance of Retention Factors 95
  4. Significant Differences between the Respondents' Assessments on the Influence and Importance of Retention Factors 98
  5. The Role of Managers in the Retention Management of the Rank-and-file Employees on the Level of Influence and the Level of Importance 99

Conclusions 101
Recommendations 105
Bibliography 107
Appendices 117
About The Author 123
Curriculum Vitae 125

LIST OF TABLES

Table 3.1. Distribution of Respondents 52
Table 3.2. Likert Scale 53
Table 4.1 Age Profile 58
Table 4.2 Gender Profile 58
Table 4.3. Marital Status Profile 59
Table 4.4. Highest Educational Attainment Profile 60
Table 4.5. Position Profile 61
Table 4.6. Hotel Classification Level 61
Table 4.7 Respondents' Years of Service in the Company 62
Table 4.8 On Level of Influence as Perceived by Managers and Rank-and-File Employees of Retention Management's Success Factors 63
Table 4.9 Retention Management's Success Factors on Level of Importance 72
Table 4.10 Retention Management's Success Factors on Level of Influence and Level of Importance 76
Table 4.11 Significant Relationship between Respondents Profiles and their Perception on the Retention Factors on the Level of Influence and Level of Importance 81
Table 4.12 Significant Relationship between Profile of Managers and their Perception on the Retention Factors 83

Table 4.13 Significant Relationship between Profile of
    Rank-and-File Employees and Their Perception on
    the Retention Factors 85
Table 4.14 Significant Difference in the Level of
    Influence of Retention Factors 87
Table 4.15 Significant Difference in the Level of
    Importance of Retention Factors 88
Table 4.16 Role of Managers in Retention Management
    of Rank-and-File Employees 90

LIST OF FIGURES

Figure 1.1. Employee Retention through relationship between Demographic Profiles & Success Factors 5

Figure 1.2. Maslow's Five Hierarchy of Needs 6

Figure 1.3. Graphical Workflow – Role of Managers in Retention Management 8

Figure 1.4. Input-Process-Output 9

CHAPTER I

THE PROBLEM AND ITS BACKGROUND

1. Introduction

The oil and gas industry crisis for the past three years imparted a worldwide termination of skilled and professional employees. It has a great impact to the oil and gas producing countries in the Middle East specifically the United Arab Emirates. This phenomenon has been of grave concern to Human Resource managers in the face of the ever-increasing high rate of employee turnover. Samuel and Chipunz (2009) observed that skilled employees made the present business landscape competitive that without them their market positioning will be in vain. The authors further stated that both the government and private corporate organizations have to rely on their human capital for competitive advantage particularly in the international market. This researcher observed that the last three years retention of hotel employees had become a difficult task for managers since these types are being terminated either due to low hotel booking or they are looking for an opportunity in some of the industry sectors for a better opportunity. As the United Arab Emirates (UAE) strived hard to get on their feet by diversifying their resources to the tourism industry, the hotel industry similarly holds their skilled and professional employees to meet the labor demands as expected in the next five years due to the incoming world event to be hosted by Dubai. It explains why some of the hotel companies are holding their employees in anticipation of the high demand of the tourism industry. Due to this imbalanced situation, the hotel industry must identify the right success factors of the strategic retention management thus reducing the frequent turnover of their employees.

Many have been written about strategic retention management as a factor of success in business. The employee-employer relationship has always been a crucial factor especially in a diverse business like the tourism and hotel industry. On the one hand, the employer exercises control and implementation of company rules and policies through managers and supervisors. They directly oversee the operations and full scheme optimization of work. On the other hand, the employees perform their respective tasks. Individually, the rank-and-file employees comprising the majority are led and managed by their direct supervisors in their leadership capacities.

When an organization loses its key employees, it loses not only the employee skills, expertise, and knowledge but also their corporate memory (Dy, 2015). Corporate memory or institutional knowledge is an abstract concept which focuses operationally on information and data, serving as a technical function in storage, retention, and security of the essential data and information that are vital for the continued long-term success and innovation for an organization (Warren, 2016).

2. The Background of the Study

The tourism and hotel industry in the UAE particularly Abu Dhabi have highly developed (Abu Dhabi Chamber of Commerce, 2016 Ed). Such position suggests that assessment of the conditions of its tourism sector should be conducted to understand better. The Supreme Council's Vision 2030 declared that it needs tourism as one of its sectors that will boost their economy than being oil dependence. Eventually, tourism and hotel industry together with the other four sectors namely, (1) transport and logistics, (2) manufacturing, (3) media, and (4) financial services and insurance were shortlisted and considered as strategic. (Retrieved from Abu Dhabi Chamber of Commerce Sectoral Report, 2016).

In 2010, the hotels that were registered in Abu Dhabi reached at 116. About 52 more hotels were added that account to a total of 168 in 2015. Such incremental development provided the hotels with the opportunity to increase their hotel guests estimated twice to 4.1 million. It produced nearly 20% growth on average during the last five years with the continuous influx in 2015 (Retrieved from Abu Dhabi Chamber of Commerce Report on Tourism and Private, April 2016, Issue 02-31032016).

The facts on the thriving tourism industry in Abu Dhabi as presented above is one of the reasons why this study is being conducted. Henceforth, its general success in the business sector will have a direct positive impact, particularly on the hotel industry. From the facts mentioned above, this research study will focus on Abu Dhabi's hotel industry that contributes to the UAE's robust economy. Since the hotel industry cannot attain its full potential by not bringing in and employing highly qualified human capital, we will now examine how the hotel management is retaining the hotel's rank-and-file employees through their role of their managers.

3. Theoretical Framework

Das and Baruah (2013) in their study on employee retention pointed out that human resources are the life-blood of any organization since it runs even the high technology-driven industry. The human capital as expressed by these authors are the most vital and dynamic resources of any organization. The acquiring of skilled and professional people even in developed economies and all areas of industries have wide stiff competition in the market. However, how developed and competitive the emerging economies are, huge, challenges and opportunities are available in the hands of these human capital. Such challenges are found to be huge that corporate organizations ae currently facing on how to retain these people. It is easier said than done to secure these people because their knowledge and skills relate to their economic competitiveness. The name of the game now is the added value of quality service let alone the insurance of profitability. No investors will invest without any good return on their investments. The bottom line of their study is really job satisfaction among employees that will result to employee retention.

A research conducted by Agyeman and Ponniah (2014) provided a model being used by the researcher as her one conceptual framework. The issue of retaining employees is not only local but universal due to human resources diversity when talking about working expatriates. Henceforth, it is one of the most challenging issues to be resolved as an opportunity. As reported by the same source, the employees' performance is the main reason why any business unit in corporate organizations should consider. A small business unit will succeed if the company could retain talented and committed employees. Their skills are the key human capital for efficient operations of the business, so much so that there is a need for designing an effective retention strategy. The authors further suggested having a retention and reward system to minimize the turnover problem. The theoretical and conceptual framework utilized by the authors in employing the various employees' demographic characteristics and their effects on turnover and retention in a small and medium unit can be a model for this research study. Since this study involves retention management employing success factors, the model will be right for this study.

Agyeman and Ponniah (2014) pointed out further that the resulting human resource practices helped minimize the turnover rate, like (1) increasing job satisfaction, (2) providing good working environment, (3) career development opportunities, and (4) increasing recognition and rewards. (Retrieved from 201https://www.researchgate.net/publication/31423 2480_Employee_Demographic_Charateristics_and_Their_Effects_on_Turnover_and_Retention_in_MSMEs.)

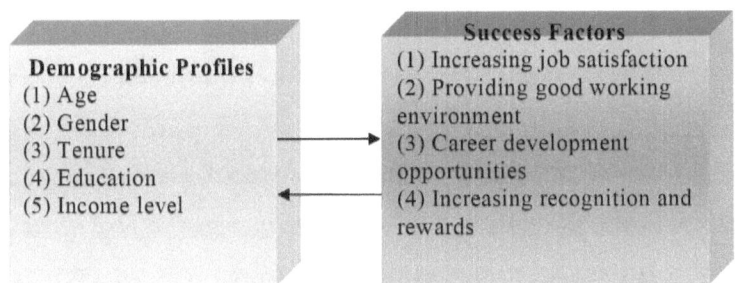

Figure 1.1. Employee Retention through relationship between Demographic Profiles & Success Factors
Source: Agyeman and Ponniah (2014)

The above-cited Figure 1.1 is a replica of the research study conducted by Agyeman and Ponniah (2014), where employees' retention banked on the demographic profiles like (1) age, (2) gender, (3) tenure, (4) education, and (5) income level in relation to the four human resource management practices such as (1) increasing job satisfaction, (2) providing good working environment, (3) career development opportunities, and (4) increasing recognition and rewards.

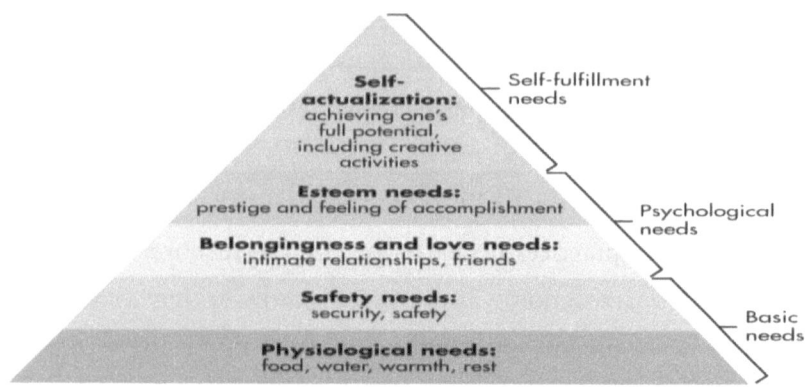

Figure 1.2. Maslow's Five Hierarchy of Needs

Figure 1.2, represents the Maslow's Theory on Five Hierarchy of Needs. It shows the three foundational elements like the (1) Basic needs, (2) Psychological needs, and the (3) Self-fulfillment needs. These three elements contain five levels such as (a) *Physiological needs* that consider food, water, warmth, and rest; (b) *Safety needs* for security and safety as the Basic needs (1); (c) *Belongingness and love needs* as for intimate relationships and friends; (d) *Esteem needs* for prestige and feeling of accomplishment as the Psychological needs (2); and (e) *Self-actualization needs* in achieving one's full potential, including creative activities considered as the Self-fulfillment needs (3).

In summary, the five hierarchical needs of Maslow can be conducted into three elements like the basic, psychological, and self-fulfillment needs.

4. Conceptual Paradigm

The researcher's concept in her study is based on the two models presented above, (1) the Agyeman and Ponniah (2014) employee retention (Figure 1.1) and the (2) Maslow's five hierarchical needs (Figure 1.2).

The Agyeman and Ponniah define management of employees through a relationship between demographic profiles and success factors while the Maslow's five hierarchy of needs defines the three elements of basic, psychological and self-fulfillment needs. It will now be the basis of the researcher's conceptual framework which is her conceptual paradigm let alone the input and the output variables. The input variables which are the independent ones will now be represented by the (A) demographic profiles consisting of the elements such as the (1) age, (2) gender, (3) marital status, (4) highest educational attainment, (5) position, (6) hotel classification, and (7) service years in the company. Another input-independent variables are the (D) strategic success factors namely, (1) recruitment and selection, (2) compensation and benefits, (3) working environment and company culture, (4) job design and work teams, (5) career development and training, (6) performance management and evaluation, and (7) communications, and (8) rewards and recognition. The (B), (C), (E), (F), & (G) factors are also presented, Figure 1.3, page 11.

The graphical workflows are shown below (Figure 1.3, page 11) with the researcher assessing the respondents' demographic profiles as to their level of influence and importance of the retention factors let alone the managers' perceptions as to their roles in the retention management of rank-and-file employees. It also shows if there will be significant differences between the respondents' assessments on the level of influence and importance of the given eight retention management factors.

As the retention management factors will be assessed as to their level of influence and level of importance using the statistical tool, it will then reveal the role of managers in the retention management of rank-and-file employees.

The process workflow made the difference in the role of the managers in the retention of management of the rank-and-file employees after both the former and the later had perceived the significant relationship between the demographic profiles and strategic success factors which the readers can see the flow in Figure 1.3.

The graphical workflow further relates the respondents' (managers and rank-and-file employees) perceptions in the relationship between the demographic profiles and the retention management strategic success factors as detailed below. It also shows the perceived level of influence and level of importance on the retention management in which the roles of the managers will play a significance in the process.

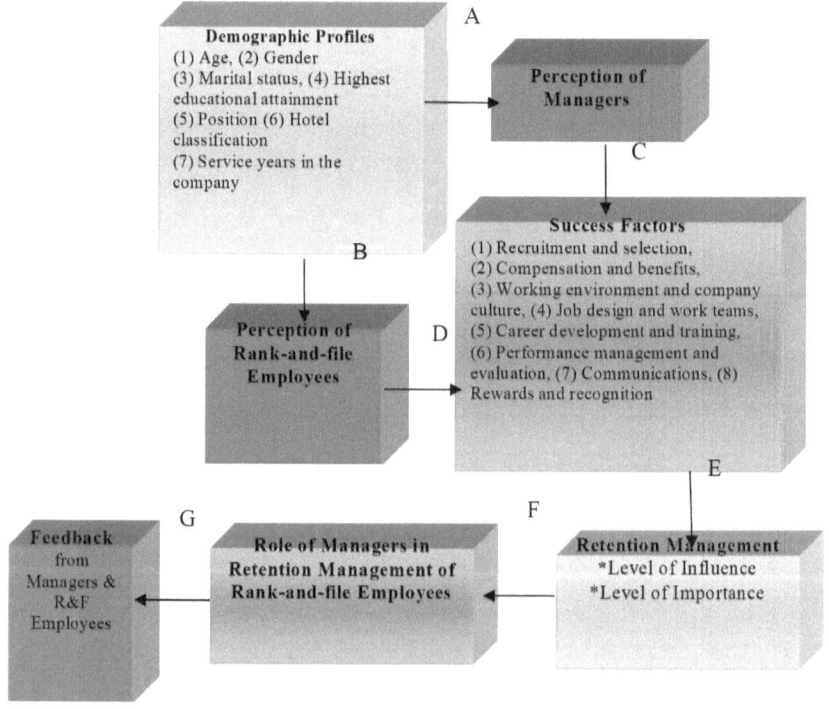

Figure 1.3. Graphical Workflow – Role of Managers in Retention Management
Source: Based on Models of (Fig 1.1) Agyeman and Ponniah, & (Fig 1.2) Maslow's Theory

As we moved forward to this research work presenting the Input-Process-Output, it is clearly shown that the independent variables (demographic profiles and success factors made a significant role resulting to the output in the role of managers in the retention process employing the research design and statistical process as you can see.

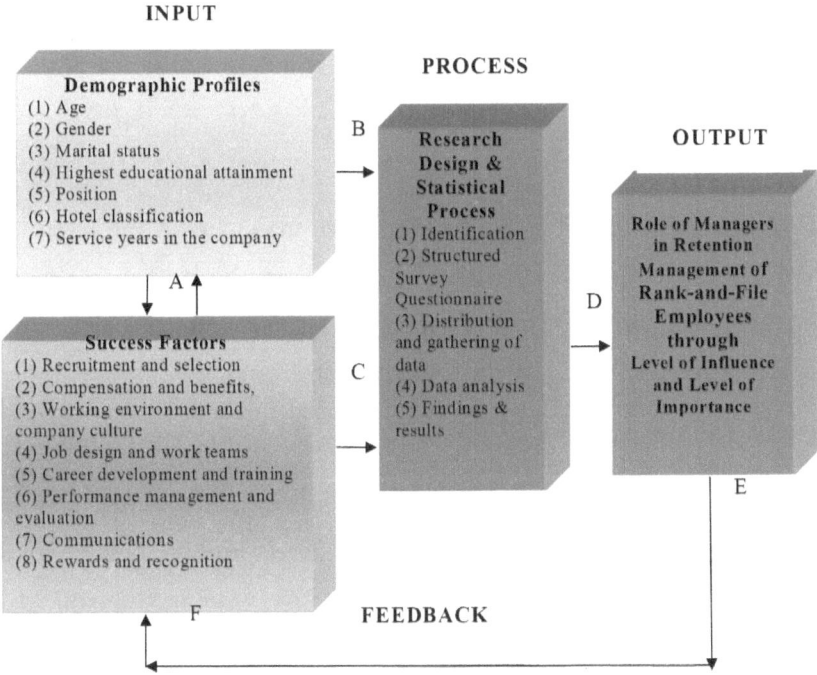

Figure 1.4. Input-Process-Output
Source: Researcher's Paradigm

5. Research Objectives

The objectives of this research study are premised on the demographic profiles of the respondents, and the respondents' assessment of the retention management's strategic success factors. The respondents' success factors significance to their level of influence and level of importance are assessed on the the significant relationship between the demographic profiles and the retention management's level of influence and level of importance. The hypothetical significant differences between the respondents' assessment of the retention management's level of influence and level of importance and the role of managers in the retention management of rank and file employees are also tested.

6. Statement of the Problem

This study aims to assess in the role of managers in the retention management of the rank-and-file employees in the level of influence and level of importance of the success factors of selected major hotels operating in Abu Dhabi of the United Arab Emirates.

Specifically, it answers to the following queries:

1. To what extent is the respondents' demographic profiles measured regarding position level, highest educational attainment, age, gender, marital status, years in the company, and hotel classification?
2. How can the respondents assess in the hotel industry's rank-and-file employees through the retention management's success factors like recruitment and selection, compensation and benefits, working environment and company culture, job design and work teams, career development and training, performance management and evaluation, communications, and rewards and recognition?
3. Are there significant relationships between the demographic profiles of the respondents and the level of influence and the level of importance of retention factors?

4. Are there significant differences in the respondents' assessment on the level of influence and level of importance of retention factors?
5. What would be the role of managers in the retention management of the rank-and-file employees in the level of influence and the level of importance of the success factors?

7. Statement of Null Hypotheses

The null hypotheses are being advanced:

1. There are no significant relationships between the demographic profiles of the respondents and the level of influence and the level importance of retention factors.
2. There are no significant differences in the assessments of the respondents in the use of the success factors for the retention of the rank-and-file employees.

8. Significance of the Study

This research study is significant for both employers and employees. The government of UAE particularly Abu Dhabi will be more interested in this study because it can give them information on the assessment of the subject case.

Those agencies that are linked with the tourism and hotel industry like the suppliers, transportation and communication industry, the public works and infrastructure agency, the food and beverage industry, and other industries and sectors will benefit from this study as the data provided will open their eyes.

The future researchers will be more interested in this study as the data provided will be a guide in their pursuit for the employers and employees relevant success factors.

The results of this study will work for higher retention of rank-and-file employees who play significant roles in the operations of selected hotels.

The government of Abu Dhabi may utilize the results of this study in formulating balanced and sustainable policies and social legislation in the growing hospitality industry, specifically on the factors affecting employment.

This study will pose an intellectual challenge to those embarking in similar fields to fill the gap between theories and practical applications in the management of hotel employees. Hotel managers will be challenged in this study, particularly on retention management.

It will also benefit the rank-and-file employees in helping managers to formulate applicable and feasible approach in their leadership and management skills

Researchers and enthusiasts may use the findings as part of their literature and baseline information in validating their studies.

This study will also credit the researcher as a contribution to the existing repository of knowledge.

9. Scope and Limitations of the Study

This study focuses on the success factors that the managers are employing through the respondents' assessment. It also focused on the role of managers in retention management of rank-and-file employees in Abu Dhabi's hotel industry. The demographic variables are being identified by the respondents. These are limited to age, gender, marital status, highest educational attainment, position and years of service in the company. The role of managers in retention management of rank-and-file employees is measured using compensation and benefits, recognition and rewards, working environment and company culture, recruitment and selection, career development and training, job design and work teams, performance management, and evaluation, and communications.

The dependent variables used are the level of influence and level of importance of the role of managers in the retention management of rank-and-file employees based on the abovementioned factors.

The researcher acknowledges that there are some weaknesses of the study which are beyond her control.

10. Definition of Terms

For purposes of clarity and better understanding, the terms that are being used throughout in this research study are operationally defined.

Career Development and Training. It refers to the continuing development of employees in their profession or career interests such as training, seminars, workshops and other related activities.

Communications. It refers to the way the employees communicate, whether oral or written. It also includes the way rank-and-file employees communicate with his/her manager, and how a manager cascades information to lower employees. It helps in the employees' way of communicating to their clients for quality service.

Compensation and Benefits. These refer to the remuneration of employees salaries and wages and benefits.

Employee Retention. It refers to the success factors being studied and assessed by the respondents that data resulted will explain how the same will be employed in the tourism and hotel industry.

<u>Job Design and Work Teams</u>. It refers to the comprehensive work or job description of the respondents along with working in teams, and how they fit themselves to work independently or in groups.

<u>Level of Importance</u>. It is defined as the factor having great significance and value to employees to stay with the company.

<u>Level of Influence</u>. Refers to the capacity of a factor to influence employee's behavior and judgment in staying with the company.

<u>Managers</u>. They are employees who are given the task of managing employees on a unit, section, department, division, and higher levels to attain the company's objectives in short-term or long-term basis.

<u>Performance Management and Evaluation</u>. It refers to management practices in measuring the employee's performance using assessment tools.

<u>Rank-and-File Employees</u>. It refers to those employees who are not performing managerial and supervisory functions.

<u>Recognitions and Rewards</u>. These are acknowledgments and awards given to employees, either monetary or non-monetary, or both.

<u>Recruitment and Selection</u>. It is the way the employee is selected or chosen among the other applicants.

<u>Retention Management</u>. It refers to the success factors being employed in this study: compensation and benefits, recognition and rewards, working environment and company culture, recruitment and selection, career development and training, job design and work teams, performance management, and evaluation, and communications.

<u>Working Environment and Company Culture</u>. It refers to the workplace or hotel, normative practices and business operations of the hotel affecting its employees.

CHAPTER II

REVIEW OF RELATED LITERATURE AND STUDIES

This chapter will review materials written about concepts that are relevant to this research work, as well as the findings of researchers who made investigations on the same field of inquiry. The readings, observations, and conclusions made by other researchers will be presented in this section for the results will support and provide this valuable study insight into the significance and implication of the subject under study. It will help the researcher in building up his conceptual framework through the given theoretical framework that resulted in the input-process-output and research paradigm. It also helps to conceptualize the research problem, formulating the research design, and designing the survey questionnaire among others.

1. Local Literature

1.1. Abu Dhabi's Travel and Tourism Industry

The Travel & Tourism Competitiveness Index 2017 shows that the UAE is considered as the most country being competitive in the Middle East and North Africa region at 29th position regarding tourism. The same source validated that its performance improved continuously with a rise of 1.4 percent since 2015. In this given statistical data, the country received 14.4 million international visitors in 2015, and an estimated more than 4 million tourists some two years ago. The country continues to offer an aggressive, friendly business environment to focus on investing the travel and tourism industry regarded as 5th, with advanced readiness in ICT as 15th and maintain its third place in the best air transport infrastructures worldwide with its connectivity and quality of their services. Moreover, it is considered as the second placer of the most secure destinations while placing 27th in a well-developed hospitality and entertainment infrastructure. (Retrieved from http://reports.weforum.org/travel-and-tourism-competitiveness-report-2017/middle-east-and-north-Africa-results/).

To further understand the hotel industry in Abu Dhabi, the need to investigate the conditions of its tourism sector, in general, was conducted. The Sectoral Report of Abu Dhabi Chamber of Commerce (2016 Ed.), profoundly observed Abu Dhabi's strategic agenda for many years particularly the tourism sector development program. Abu Dhabi's Supreme Council declared Abu Dhabi's Vision 2030 that the country needs tourism as among some sectors that will steer the economy away from its oil dependence. Further, the sector was shortlisted with the other four other sectors as strategic in the current five-year business plan, namely, transport and logistics, manufacturing, media, and financial services and insurance. (Abu Dhabi Chamber of Commerce Sectoral Report, 2016).

The same source stated that it is with certainty that the tourism industry concerning hospitality-related businesses plays a significant and critical role in the country's economic diversification program as well as in the development of the private sector. About 90 percent of the tourism activities in the country were already accounted for in the private sector. It puts the sector in the lead position in its tourism development. It is expected that the revenues for the government will be provided in different directions. The earlier report of visitors provided that nearly 1.4 million visitors in 2015 in Abu Dhabi by the Tourism and Cultural Authority of Abu Dhabi throughout the UAE; hotels have multiplied. This kind of phenomenon in Abu Dhabi will support the influx of the business; likewise the rest and recreation tourists (Abu Dhabi Chamber of Commerce Sectoral Report, 2016).

The reported hotels in 2010 were registered at 116 specifically in Abu Dhabi. An additional of 52 hotel establishments which jumped the numbers to 168 in 2015 were recorded. Such incremental development provided the hotels the opportunity to increase their hotel guests estimated twice to 4.1 million. It produced nearly 20% growth on average during the last five years with the continuous influx in 2015 (Abu Dhabi Chamber of Commerce Report on Tourism and Private, April 2016, Issue 02-31032016).

The above data shows a relatively successful tourism industry in Abu Dhabi. Its success let alone the business sector, in general, will mainly have a direct positive impact on the hotel industry. This research work will focus on the Abu Dhabi hotel industry identifying several success factors that contribute to the country's economy and the relevance of the human capital to be retained that promotes this success namely, the managers, and rank-and-file employees.

1.2. Abu Dhabi's Flagship Projects

Abu Dhabi's key flagship projects are part of the country's development program, in which one of these is the Louvre Abu Dhabi which opened in the middle of 2016, one of the world-class tourist destinations. By this initiative, tourism clinched its critical role in the country's economic development program as a substitute for their oil and gas dependence.

About 90% of tourism projects are accounted for by the private sector in Abu Dhabi. It puts them in the lead position.

However, Abu Dhabi occupies a low rank at 88th place with 2 million arrivals in 2013. France at 80 million visitors in 2013 leads the list. The United States of America followed it at 75 million in 2014. Dubai was in 12th place with 10.5 million arrivals in 2013. Mecca followed this at 7.5 million in the same year. (World Trade Organization's Tourism Barometer.

Abu Dhabi's ambitious target for 2030 is somewhat unusual. It will be four times the number of arrivals in 2013 for a whopping eight million visitors per year. It is highly ambitious but in all intent reasonable because of Dubai's success and current plans for several high-profile projects.

Abu Dhabi's GDP in 2014 was closed to 5.5 percent and ended up at more than 8 percent of GDP considering the factors in the supplying sectors. However, this includes Dubai's thriving tourism sector. (Report from World Travel and Tourism Council Analysis).

The tourism sector's size for Abu Dhabi alone is smaller compared with the rest of Abu Dhabi's economy. About 1 percent of GDP and 2 percent of the non-oil economy is the sector's direct contribution if a combined of other services with arts and recreation are considered a proxy for tourism. If it includes tourism-related transport services, the share of total GDP might increase to around 2% (Abu Dhabi Chamber of Commerce Sectoral Report, 2016).

The Abu Dhabi's tourism industry just recently has slackened as gross value added dropped 5.6% in 2014 while the data for 2015 have not yet been published. The arts and recreation services contributed to the decline while making the food and accommodation at status quo from 2013. It was also reported that the industry remain stagnated that resulted in a lesser reduction in 2015, although, these are just estimates and trying to confirm.

As the oil price slide and its neighbors' related effects made some negative factors, the largest share of visitors provided by its neighbors made some impact. The global and regional economic trends made Abu Dhabi's tourism industry in a disadvantaged position. It was due to the fact that in the fourth-quarter of 2014, the strength of the US dollars against the euro and most major emerging-market currencies, including the Chinese yuan as well as the Russian money, the tourists planned on their rest and recreation in Abu Dhabi were considered more expensive than from Europe and most Asian countries.

About 280,000 visitors from India or a share of 7% were registered in Abu Dhabi while followed by the United Kingdom and China. The tourist flows from all major countries except for Germany that posted double-digit growth rates from 2014. The reasons for this low growth were the emerging markets' lesser growth, the unstable oil rates, and the stability of the US dollar and the dirham, respectively. In line with this argument, it is safely concluded that the tourist flows would have grown faster even in given global circumstances. The Russian tourists in 2015 reduced to half with the 2014 data due to the country's financial weakness and the country's recession crisis although their tourists have not played some significant role in the previous years ranking at 20th among the top source countries for Abu Dhabi in 2014 which is a considerable contrast with Dubai where their tourists were more significant.

Reports showed that the arrivals at Abu Dhabi International Airport marked a new record in passenger traffic at 23 million. These were combined arrivals and departures in 2015, which provide clues about the geographical origin of Abu Dhabi visitors. The GCC countries travelers are much less strongly represented for obvious reasons, but arrivals from outside the GCC warned that non-Arab Asia is playing a critical role, with more than 4 million passengers in 2014. The report showed that it almost doubles the 2010 figure. It is impressive to note that the traveler numbers from Europe have grown faster which accounted for more arrivals at 2.3 million in 2014. (Retrieved from http://reports.weforum.org/travel-and-tourism-competitive-ness-report-2017/country-profiles/#economy=ARE).

Establishments of the Abu Dhabi hotels have grown faster in recent years to accommodate the swelling flow of business and leisure travelers. About 116 hotel establishments were registered in Abu Dhabi in 2010 which continued to leap in 2015 to 168 an additional of 52. Accordingly, the hotel guests swelled to more than doubled to 4.1 million. This data showed nearly 20% on average during the last five years and continue to surge in 2015.

Abu Dhabi continues to attract a diverse range of internationally recognized hoteliers. One of these hoteliers is a local private developer, Bin Otaiba Investment Group, in partnership with the Hilton group to operate a resort. Such partnership activities are regarded as a standard business model for Abu Dhabi. Investment in this type is funded by both the government-related entities and local private investors. The hotels are operated by high-profile brands considering such names as Grand Hyatt, Four Seasons, Edition, Fairmont, Biltmore, and Hard Rock Hotel to name a few.

1.3. Abu Dhabi's Hotel Industry

As the hotels were developed in all significant classifications, some of these luxury segments lead. Although the oil prices declined, and the weaker outlook was seen, more related projects are either in the pipeline or under construction. Two of the luxury segment's performers like the Grand Hyatt and Hard Rock Hotel undergoes their development which is considered critical on their status. The focus on continuous tourism growth in Abu Dhabi are manifestations of the Emirate's expectations that business travel activities are increasing. The price war competition did not deter the hotels' resolved although the average room revenue already gone to their bottom rates although the luxury segment found its rescue amazing. It shows a robust incremental capacity growth and the revenue per available room (RevPAR), was relatively stable between 2011 and 2015, with a steady increase of an average occupancy rate hitting at 75% in 2015.

As reported, the average room revenue declined steadily to 11% from 2011 to 2015. With the additional room capacity to the market, this trend will add fuel to the price war unless more quests are coming into Abu Dhabi to have their business, and rest recreation spent and maintained for a certain period.

It is a known fact that travelers focused on the luxury category staying in the five-star hotel particularly from the UAE, Europe, and North America. This demand increased in 2014. Although in the recent past, thirty percent visitors from the non-Arab Asia and Africa stayed in that luxurious category, while most of these visitors preferred the three or four-star hotels or hotel apartments. It was also noted that tourists from the Asia countries and the UAE shifted their choice to the luxury segment making an increase for five-star rooms between 7 to 10 percent. Eventually, price effects might play a significant role as the offered lower costs can attract travelers to upgrade to the luxury segment.

The need for a high-quality infrastructure is critical to this issue at hand. It will ensure sufficient capacity to cater to the surging number of travelers. In line with this viewpoint, Etihad Airways has actively contributed to the increase in the tourism industry. By 2025, this Abu Dhabi flag carrier which has less than years in its operations has the vision of expanding its network to a worldwide destination of 160. In the end, Abu Dhabi tourism will undoubtedly benefit from such a source of travelers. Such growth of the Etihad Airways provided the Abu Dhabi International Airport (AUH) the opportunity to be considered as one of the world's leading airports concerning passenger traffic expansion, ranking fourth from the country like Thailand, Turkey, and China. The opening of the Midfield Terminal at Abu Dhabi International Airport, which was currently targeted for opening on National Day 2017, (which at the current year 2018 while this research is being prepared) will be able to receive 30 million passengers per year. So far, the researcher has not got any data regarding the opening of the new airport.

With the advent of a new port terminal as an additional service to the air transport system, Abu Dhabi constructed a new cruise ship terminal at Mina Zayed. Opened in January 2016, an estimated less than a quarter of a million ate expected to arrive during the year. Eventually, it will underscore Abu Dhabi as a landmark for cruise ship tourism in the Arabian Gulf. The researcher at this moment, do not have any data as to the total number of passengers in 2016 being accommodated.

Another tourism facility currently being developed is the first cruise beach stopover at Sir Bani Yas Island. It will help diversify shore excursion opportunities. In addition to the above flagship projects, the lodging facilities for business travel is in place. Taking an active role as a business tourism destination, the Abu Dhabi Convention Bureau is also putting more emphasis on its completion in accordance to plan. (Tourism and Cultural Authority). All these initiatives have produced tangible results. Accordingly, it brought Abu Dhabi into the top 100 busiest cities for global meeting destinations (International Congress and Convention Association's Rankings). ADNEC estimated that the economic impact of business events to reach AED 5.1 billion by 2020, with an average 7 percent increase annually (Tourism and Cultural Authority and Abu Dhabi National Exhibition Centre (ADNEC)).

Since 2010, several high-profile tourist and leisure attraction have either opened their gates or are currently being developed and built in Abu Dhabi. The Ferrari World on Yas Island was one of them. It began in 2010. At that time, actual demand did not quite match the relatively high expectations and capacity. The theme park has been consolidated and established itself as a critical item to be considered a world-class tourist attraction.

In the Saadiyat Island, the most important projects currently being developed were located at the three central districts. The project was kicked-off in 2007 with its conception some decade ago, Saadiyat Island will be hosting 3 in 1 service district such as a beach, a cultural, and a marina. Based on a master plan, the 27-square-kilometer area was developed and in progress. It involves vital elements namely a combination of living (residential villas and apartments), world-class cultural and world-class tourism (two five-star beach hotels already in place, a golf club, shopping).

Now in place, is a whole range of other tourist attractions scattered across the country. A zoning strategy is being developed for better overview and facilitation let alone access to all facilities. It will encourage tourists to visit more facilities and eventually lengthen their overall stay in the country. It divides Abu Dhabi into several distinctive tourism areas, to provide the visitors or tourists the edge in their tour package cost wise and fun. (Abu Dhabi Tourism and Culture Authority report).

The UAE had improved its visa procedures for 142 countries during 2010–14. One good example is China, with an MOA in 2012 to provide service benefits for holders of diplomatic, service, and special passports from the mutual exemption of visas to enter both countries. As this developed, China which accounted for just 4% of travelers to Abu Dhabi from 2010 to 2014, currently the guest count leaped 166% and 47% in 2014 and 2015, respectively.

Chinese travelers, while providing an excellent visiting agreement spent only the shortest stay among all major visitor nations for one and half day. In contrast, travelers from the United States, the United Kingdom, and Germany, usually stayed an average of more than four days.

The UAE was highly rated as second regarding economic freedom and ease of doing business, and first in the Middle East region (The World Bank report). According to the World Economic Forum, the UAE ranked 24th and leads the Middle East region on its travel and tourism competitiveness globally (Global Travel and Tourism Competitiveness Index in 2015). This recognition covers safety and security, hygiene, international openness, transportation infrastructure, and culture resources, which are particularly relevant for the tourism industry (Global Travel and Tourism Competitiveness Index in 2015).

The tourism in Abu Dhabi, like any other global tourist destination, will depend on what visitors are able and prepared to spend. The outlook could be brighter with global growth stagnating and growth in emerging markets, especially China, shows slowing down. The trends in oil-price will play a critical role in the outlook of Abu Dhabi's tourism industry whether the recent weak patch will continue and transform into long-term stagnation and decline. The reason for these trends is that the GCC countries are still the largest source of tourist origins.

That scenario might not be favorable at this current situation unless the price of oil stays very low for an extended time. On the one hand, considering the demand side of the tourism market, visitors from GCC countries will trim and manage expenses more closely because those economies will be adjusting to the new environment of low oil prices. On the other hand, other countries, such as China and India, might pick up some of the slack.

It is viewed positively that Abu Dhabi will climb steadily to a more attractive international tourism spot with more tourism attractions in the pipeline. The travelers from non-Arab Asia can make the difference where substantial growth can be seen in the near term (Abu Dhabi Chamber of Commerce Report on Tourism and Private, April 2016, Issue 02-31032016).

2. Literature/Studies

2.1. Demographic Profiles

In this section, profiles such as age, marital status, highest educational attainment, work position, hotel classification, and years of service in the company will be briefly presented for the sake of providing the readers a bird's eye view and its relationship to the research study. The profiles as part of the independent variables will be briefly discussed.

2.2. Age Profile

Age, as everybody knows reflects all the changes that occur in a person's life stages (Clarke and Korotchenko, 2011).) which is relevant to the person's history. First, the person has to pass through the incubation stage, then to growth and development, followed by maturity, and the last stage is declination until his lifespan ended. (Vecchio, 1993), opined that the leaders' and followers' aging might have an impact on how the leaders lead effectively and how the followers followed objectively. It means that any person at a mature age can decide to do the good and bad thing as the situation warrants. This research study found out that 70 percent are from 30 to 49 years old, while 18 to 29 years old at 21 percent and 50 and above years old at 8 percent.

2.3. Gender Profile

Thackray & McCall, (1997) in their article observed that the male gender occupies the leadership position in any organization. Women of today found their lead role in some of the entrepreneur endeavors. Basing from this trend, more women hold the position as observed in the Philippines. Astin and Leland, (1991) supported this viewpoint and found out how committed, a passion for justice and equality, and their willingness to take risks prompted remarkable achievements, from creating women's re-entry programs in higher education to pressing for legislation to combat sex discrimination in the workplace. In this particular study, 59 percent represent the male gender while 41 percent for the female gender.

2.4. Marital Status

Married employees in different hotels of Abu Dhabi comprise most respondents at 55 percent. The rest at 45 percent are represented by widowed at 3 percent, single parent at 10 percent, and only 32 percent. This profile as observed can be one of the categories selected by the researcher since it can support her study when considering a significant relationship between the demographic profiles and the success factors in retention management.

2.5. Highest Educational Attainment

The college graduates are the majority of respondents at 60 percent. The rest are undergraduates at 16 percent, master's degree at 20 percent, and Ph.D. degrees at 3 percent. Macasa, Jr. (2018) in his dissertation cited Director (2016), Bush & Middlewood (2013), Haytt & De Ciantis (2012), Winston (2009), Aquino (2004), Zaleznik (2001), & Pankid (1999), and pointed out that education provides a unique and management challenge geared in potential human development. The cited authors further pointed out that it is the role of the person's calling, competence, confidence, and character that serves as guide and inspiration for the person to persistently heed them to attain his objective. Such endeavors will develop a person into a leader.

2.6. Work Position

A more significant majority of the respondents at 81 percent occupy positions on the rank-and-file level while the others are managers at 19 percent. As observed, this researcher knows that most of the persons employed in the hotel industry are in the rank-and-file status while those working as managers are less.

2.7. Hotel Classification

Most of the hotels where the respondents are currently employed are classified as 5-Star hotel at 47 percent, 4-Star at 39 percent and 3-Star at

14 percent. It is the researcher's observation that most of the respondents want to work in a 5-Star hotel for more remuneration to receive and at the same token more tips are in the offing.

2.8. Years of Service in the Company

Most of the respondents at 38 percent served between 2 to 5 years, 28 percent below, two years, and over five years at 33 percent. It is the researcher's observation that the respondents tend to hop between hotel on a certain period to find out for themselves which type of hotel can provide better greener pasture.

3. Retention Management

Keeping employees with a corporate organization is not an assurance to stay until retirement. However, retaining an employee until his/her end of service has completed will both benefit the employer and the employee. The concept of retention is a complex initiative between both parties, the employer and the employee. The manager has a role in it while the Human Resource unit has the policy to follow. According to Zineldin (2000), there is no single recipe for retaining an employee in a corporate organization. There will be a policy on this initiative in which the employee has to follow and ensure that he/she has read and internalize all the employment rules and act for his benefit and the sound and development of the company. The author further explains that retention has been viewed as a kind of obligation that the employee has to undertake with an exchange for remuneration continuously.

Another author pointed out that retention can be defined as (1) customer liking, (2) identification, (3) commitment, and (4) trust, which are considered as emotional-cognitive retention constructs. The other two definitions for retention are the (5) readiness to recommend, and (6) repurchase intentions, which are considered behavioral intentions (Stauss et al., 2001).

Logan (2000) on his research study opined that several vital factors drive retention and to be consistently managed like (1) organizational culture, (2) communication, (3) strategy, (4) pay and benefits, (5) flexible work schedule and (6) career development systems. These critical factors if not well managed by the unit managers based on the HR policies and roles might ignite demotivation among the employees resulting in an unproductive action by both the employer and the employees. Further, the author explained that the increased organization mergers and acquisitions made employees unhappy because they felt vulnerable to an unsecured job. On the one hand, taking into consideration Maslow's five hierarchical needs, the employee must bring his/her strategic career initiative to guarantee employment for security needs. On the other hand, an employer needs to keep their employee from leaving or going to work for other companies since it will be more expensive for a fast turnover than employee retention. The author concluded that a company that offers employee development programs are finding success with retaining workers. The researcher on her part experienced that a hotel establishment will spend more on activities associated with hiring and retraining new employees.

Eskildesen & Nussler (2000) in their article surmised that good help is hard to find, that at this current trend, it is even harder these days than ever before because the job market is becoming increasingly tight. Davidow & Utah (1989) impressed their readers that wooing existing employee through employee development or talent management programs costs less than acquiring new talents, as organization knows their employee, their personal needs, while no more additional cost will be expended. Denton (2000) admonished that employees who are happy with their jobs are more devoted to doing a quality service and look forward to improving their organizational customers' satisfaction. Accordingly, employees who are satisfied have higher intentions of continuing with their organization, which prevents turnover rate (Mobley et al., 1979).

Retention initiative should be linked between satisfaction and behavioral intentions so that both employer and employee will have their mutual trust that could bring benefit to both parties (Anderson & Sullivan, 1993). The employee's involvement as highly significant could enhance the employer's retention process (Arthur, 1994).

In summary, the literature as mentioned above in retention defines as the continuing relationship between the employee and their organization. It means that a satisfied employee will likely behave as one of the owners of the organization that he/she will commit his/her whole life to work until retirement.

Dinora et al. (2017) in their study, the Impact of Customer Relationship Management on Customer Loyalty, Customer Retention and Customer Profitability for Hotelier Sector explained that the entrance of strategies oriented to marketing relational in Hotelier Sector had changed the traditional way of travel agents and other representatives arranging hospitality services for hotel and travel reservations. Loyalty marketing is one strategy that the authors conducted in their study. This is one new area where the hotel is making opportunity with constant enhancement for their benefits. The conduct of this process allows the hoteliers to prepare a related guest programs, while enhancing their services and promotions tailored to the hotel guest preferences. This data in turn as collected can be used in identifying the needs of particular customers across hotel chains It then enable to use marketing that can be targeted at specific groups of people. Opportunities are then provided in evaluating frequent guest programs, service personalization, and trend analysis performances by the hotel management. This relational marketing program is used to collect data of guest information and transaction allowing hoteliers to see target groups for marketing. These transactions will result in creating and managing guest loyalty programs and reward schemes. The authors conducted this study for the purpose of finding the impact relationship between effective customer relationship implementation, customer loyalty, and customer retention and customer profitability. The results add value to three-stars hotels in Mexico, and provide some invaluable statistical results essential for hotel managers and owners to successfully enhance customer loyalty, customer retention and customer profitability.

Perception of frontline employees towards career growth opportunities: implications on turnover intention

Ohunakin et al., (2018) observed in their study "Perception of frontline employees towards career growth opportunities: implications on turnover intention," that retaining their talented employees has become a major challenge confronting the management in hospitality industry. They likewise observed that researchers from different climes have advocated for adequate retention strategies. These involve career growth opportunities just for overcoming the alarming rate of employees' turnover in hotel organizations. However, there was a gap of empirical study between career growth opportunities and employees' turnover intention. The authors further stated that in filling the gap, quantitative data were gathered with 327 copies of questionnaire, administered to the frontline employees working in twenty-two 5-star hotels in Nigeria. The researchers used the Structural equation modelling (SEM) in testing the hypothesis, with descriptive statistics, path analysis, maximum likelihood estimates and goodness of fit indices. The results revealed that all the parameters for career growth opportunities used in this study, inversely interact with turnover intention among the respondents. The findings show that organizations should pay adequate attention to career goal progress, professional ability development, promotion speed and remuneration growth of their talented employees. It implies that, these factors are pivotal for saving the cost of hiring new entrants, reduce the rate of turnover intention/actual turnover, and retain experienced high performers in hotel industry. The result of the research established the effects of career growth opportunities on turnover intention in Nigerian context.

4. Strategic Human Resource Management

An overview of the elements of the strategic human resources will be presented in this section that will support this research work regarding the working environment and company culture, job design and work teams, career development training, performance management, and evaluation, and communications.

The role of human resource management as an interpreter of the policy in improving organizational performance and acquire competitive advantage using human capital (employee) that provide quality service (efficient and effective) is the focus of the strategic human resource management (SHRM) (Wright and Snell, 1991). Wright and McMahan (1992) classified SHRM as a guide of human resource allocations and activities to enable the organization to achieve its goals. Accordingly, it involves a corresponding relationship between human resource management and corporate strategy (Gilani, Zadeh & Saderi, 2012).

5. Recruitment and Selection

As an implementing guide for the corporate to sustain and operate using the human capital, SHRM needs a fundamental characteristic for having a fit, which means the utilization of human resources to help with the achievement of organization goals (Wright and McMahan, 1992). The authors further defined the two types of fit, e.g., a vertical fit and straight fit. The vertical fit on one hand as described by Schuler and Jackson (1987), involves the alignment of human resource management policies and practices and the organization's other functional strategies which was viewed as a critical step towards ultimate corporate goal achievement. The straight fit, on the other hand, was first defined by Baird and Meshoulam (1988) implies alignment and congruence among the various HRM practices and was identified by Wei (2006) as systems, processes, and rewards.

6. Employee Engagement

Bhatnagar, (2007) in her study indicated that a good level of engagement might lead to high retention, but only for a limited time in the Information Technology (ITES) sector. The study indicated a need for a more rigorous employee engagement construct and practical implications for retention in the BPO/ITES sector. The results pointed out in the expected direction, and the research aims were fulfilled. The first phase low factor loadings indicated low engagement scores at the beginning of the career and completion of 16 months with the organization. The high factor loadings at intermediate stages of employment showed a high engagement level, but the interview data reflected that this might mean high loyalty, but only for a limited time. The second phase factor loadings showed three distinct factors like organizational culture, career planning along with incentives, and corporate support. The first two were indicative of high attrition.

7. Working Environment and Company Culture

Deery (2008) in her study focused on job attitudes like job satisfaction and organizational commitment, and personal attributes like positive and negative affectivity, the role of work-life balance (WLB) in employee turnover and, finally, the strategies provided to alleviate high turnover rates. The author recommends the need for legislation on maximum, as well as minimum working hours, good role models at the workplace, flexible working hours and arrangements, sound recruitment and training opportunities and company family-friendly work policies.

8. Job Design and Work Team

On job design, Daniels et al. (2017) in their study investigated the role of other employment practices, either as instruments for job redesign or as instruments that augment job redesign. It focused on the employee's well-being considering performance as an outcome by reviewing thirty-three intervention studies. The author's finding shows that well-being and performance may be improved by training workers in enhancing their jobs, redesign the job, and comprehensive approaches to the existing system by way of strengthening job design and a range of other employment practices. Insufficient evidence concerning the effects of training managers in job redesign to make any firm conclusions and participatory approaches to improving job design have mixed results. The author concluded that successful implementation of interventions should be associated with worker involvement and engagement, managerial commitment and integration with other organizational systems.

On the teamwork, McEwan et al. (2017) conducted a systematic review and meta-analysis of teamwork interventions using a controlled experimental design by way of literature search returned 16,849 unique articles to improve teamwork and team performance. The finding shows positive and significant medium-sized effects for teamwork interventions on both collaboration and team performance. Moderator analyses were also conducted, which generally revealed positive and significant impact concerning several samples, intervention, and measurement characteristics. Balanced against the contributions and insights provided by the various moderator analyses conducted in this study, the overall take-home message is that teamwork training is an effective way to foster teamwork and team performance. These effects appear to be evident across a range of samples, utilizing numerous intervention methods, and when considering various measurement characteristics. Interventions appear to be particularly useful when they target multiple dimensions of teamwork and include experiential activities for team members to actively learn about, practice, and continually develop collaboration.

9. Career Development and Training

Yahya and Go (2002) in their study examine the linkages between human resource management and knowledge management. It will explore the association between the four areas of human resource management with the five areas of knowledge management. On the one hand the four areas of human resource management include (1) training, (2) decision-making, (3) performance appraisal, and

(4) compensation and reward. On the other hand, the five areas of knowledge management consist of (1) knowledge acquisition, (2) knowledge documentation, (3) knowledge transfer, (4) knowledge creation, and (5) knowledge application. The result based on the statistic suggests that a knowledge organization requires a different management approach than the non-knowledge organization. It shows that the SHRM role is also unique. For the development of employees, the authors likewise suggested placing the focus on (1) achieving quality, (2) creativity, (3) leadership, and (5) problem-solving skill. The authors further suggested the correct application of the design compensation and reward system by (1) promoting group performance, (2) knowledge sharing, and (3) innovative thinking. The bases in the evaluation of employee's knowledge management practices and an input for directing knowledge management efforts should put to task the performance appraisal system.

10. Performance Management and Evaluation

Osmania et al. (2012) in their article surmised that an organization's human resources are of great importance to its success. Without active employees, organizations would work so ineffective and would risk failing to enforce claims of its objectives and mission. Therefore, every organization within the strategy that has, it applies the most appropriate system of performance management, a process that helps in the commitment of all employees towards achieving the objectives of the organization.

Further in their study, if employees see that they are evaluated with their work and commitment, then this will result to motivate them to work harder. As a component related to performance evaluation, it would play an essential role in motivating employees. It will stimulate them as their salary will increase as well receive other forms of rewards such as appreciation/gratitude, praise, etc. Therefore, many international organizations or institutions within their organizational structure apply the method of the remuneration as a result of the excellent performance of their employees. The authors further stated that this kind of approach could be used elsewhere since the performance assessment process is seen as something more formal and must necessarily be accomplished by the leaders, where in most cases is done the subjective evaluation of left out without assessing the real capabilities and results of employee performance. The application of the method of remuneration as a result of the excellent performance of employees in public institutions can be a matter of choice because often-times the assessment is subjective and related to narrow personal or political according to management department or institution's political leaders. Also, an element that must be present in the evaluation of performance in other countries is to focus more attention on finding and application of methods for improving performance, rather than just their use without any positive result. It is suggested that in the future to organize workshops, conferences, roundtables and sessions aimed at different training and awareness of the reviewers of the importance of human resources, and the importance of assessing the value and contribution they provide that are propulsive towards a most successfully future of the organization or institution.

Sanderson (2002) in his article pointed out that public sector reforms in the UK produced a new model of open governance throughout OECD member states. It focused on performance management with the country doing a modest role. The author explained that the development of this program had been primarily 'top-down' with focus on control and 'upwards accountability' rather than promoting learning and improvement. Performance review and evaluation quoted are focused on this program in modernizing local government offices as a prime mover of continuous improvement in promoting the best value. Recent research showed that there is uneven capacity for evaluation in local government let alone found out many obstacles to evaluation exist in organizational cultures. The author suggested that to achieve the purpose of the best value; the local authorities need to get out of the box thus ensuring that the capacity for evaluation and learning is embedded as an attribute of 'culture.'

Several citations on the above article by different researchers were posted to support Sanderson's research on performance management and evaluation and communication as well as their posting in the bibliography such as follows: Aversano et. al, (2017) (Outcome-Based Performance Management in Public Sector), Rensburg and Mapitsa (2017) (Methodological reflections), Alach (2017) (the use of performance measurement in universities), Mitchell & Berlan (2017) (Evaluation in non-profit organization), Laihonen et. al, (2017) (Strategic knowledge management and evaluating local government), Rojas (2016) (Performance measurement and management control), Smith, et. al., (2016) (High performance in health care priority setting), Purnamasari (2016) (Concept similarity searching for support query), Sneider et. al., (2016) (Barriers and facilitators to evaluation of health policies and programs).

Blalock (1999) in her article pointed out the integration of evaluation research and performance management movement needs coordination and close integration to ensure that the goals of information production are completely followed and sees to it that the primary concept, measurement, and methodological problems are integrated. The research work provides suggestions on how these two essential approaches can incorporate professionally and organizationally. Such an initiative can serve the purpose of enhancing the reliability and validity of social program assessments, and therefore for improving policy development and program management. Similarly, in this article (integration of evaluation and performance management), there are quite some citations posted in the bibliography which are not published on this page.

Tansuhaj (1988) emphasized in her article that employee plays a central role in attracting, building and maintaining relationships with customers in services marketing. The internal marketing programs are focused on strongly oriented employee development; therefore, it has to recognize the central role of employees in service marketing. The author further stated in exploring the linkage between internal marketing activities which are directed at employee recruitment, training, motivation, communication, and retention and the more traditional external marketing activities, e.g., pricing, advertising, and personal selling. The author concluded that service managers could enhance customer loyalty, satisfaction and perception of quality after examination of the relationship between the critical elements of the services marketing management model comprise of internal and external marketing, employee attitudes and behavior, and customer attitudes and behavior. This article was cited by several researchers who are not posted on this page but were posted in the bibliography.

11. Communication

Cohn (2007) in his article pointed out that effective communication requires paying attention to an entire process, not just the content of the message. When you are the messenger in this process, you should consider potential barriers at several stages that can keep your intended audience from receiving your signal. Be aware of how your attitudes, emotions, knowledge, and credibility with the receiver might impede or alter whether and how your message is received. Be mindful of your body language when speaking. Consider the attitudes and knowledge of your intended audience as well. Diversity in age, sex, and ethnicity or race add to the communication challenges, as do different training backgrounds. Individuals from different cultures may assign very different meanings to facial expressions, use of space, and, especially, gestures. For example, in some Asian cultures, women learn that it is disrespectful to look people in the eye and so they tend to have downcast eyes during a conversation. But in the United States, this body language could be misinterpreted as a lack of interest or a lack of attention.

The author further stated that in choosing the right medium for the message you want to communicate. E-mail or phone call? Personal visit? Group discussion at a meeting? Notes in the margin or a typed review? Sometimes more than one medium is appropriate, such as when you give the patient written material to reinforce what you have said, or when you follow-up a telephone conversation with an e-mail beginning, "As we discussed.…"

As the author further elaborated that for one-on-one communication, the setting and timing can be critical to communicating effectively. Is a chat in the corridor OK, or should this be a closed-door discussion? In your office or over lunch? Consider the mindset and milieu of the communication receiver. Defer giving complex information on someone's first day back from vacation or if you are aware of situations that may be anxiety-producing for that individual. Similarly, when calling someone on the phone, ask initially if this is a convenient time to talk. Offer to set a specific time to call back later.

The author concluded that organizing the content of the message is a must if you want to communicate. Make sure the information you are trying to convey is not too complicated or lengthy for either the medium you are using or the audience. Use language appropriate for the audience. With patients, avoid medical jargon.

12. Other Factors Affecting Employee Retention

The factors affecting employee retention needs to be studied as these will deter the growth and development of the corporate organizations (Agrela et al., 2008). Another research study (Gale Group, 2006) suggests that retention strategies should be effectively adapted to ongoing organizational change that will adequately satisfy the needs of all employees. They further explained that in redefining modern retention strategies, the traditional salary and benefits package have to be revisited (Gale Group, 2006), as well as compensation (Feldman, 2000) embracing employee motivation (Thomas, 2000), as crucial factors to cater to the diversity and extended stay of the workforce in the organization. Authority, (2009) opined that retention factors should consider the needs and desires of employees at any age, and enhance the levels of individual job satisfaction, loyalty, and commitment. Cunningham (2002) added some success factors to harness retention management like employee's rank with equivalent employee's recognition and providing flexibility and training as top priorities for the individual to permanently stay until retirement. Moreover, Walker (2001) and other experts suggested that for employee retention to succeed, a supportive learning and working climate should be given direct attention by the management. Further, some list of attributes was being suggested by the authors such as career development (Authority, 2009), organizational commitment (Owens, 2006), communication (Gopinath and Becker, 2000) and superior-subordinate relationship (Zenger, et.al, 2000) which are also the factors known for prolonged stay of the employees in the organization.

Griffeth et al., (2000) observed that the list of employee retention factors is based on the theoretical frameworks cited from published articles. The variables being used might not be practical but testing the relative frequency with various retention factors employed to get the resulting data of the employees' versions for their retention. For additional information of the readers on retention management, this researcher suggests reading the work of Yazinski, (2009) which provide a brief introduction and review of the 12 retention factors working towards the preservation of an organization's most valuable asset, the employees.

13. Compensation and Benefits

Compensation is a yardstick of a person's struggle for a decent life. When applying for a job in any corporate organization either public or government, the person's line of focus is on the total remuneration he/she can place in his/her pocket every month. Although sometimes we will not be aware of this matter-of-factly situation, it is the human instinct that put a person in such a desperate position. Why? Because that is the fundamental or basic needs of a person as provided by Maslow's theory of five hierarchical needs. As the person climbs to the next level until he gets on the top of the hierarchy, then that basic needs will not anymore be focused but something which is more than the fundamental, self-actualization.

The situation of our current president in the Philippines could be more relating to this situation. So many times did he stated that his monthly salary is just enough for what he needs. Imagine a person in authority and the highest official of the land does not require any recognition and awards except that he is just a government official doing the daily routine job as president. What a humble man and the only president the researcher have known in her life that will be a legacy and icon of the Filipino people if not all.

In a nutshell, benefits can clearly show employees that a company is either trustworthy and committed. Most of the employees choose to stay in the company if they believe that their life will always be on top of the world. This line of thinking is not that ideal but something a fairy tale. However, some companies owe their successes to the employees so much so that their supporters are focused on their welfare. Lochhead and Stephens, (2004) opined that there are facts to suggest when talking about compensation and benefits. Accordingly, these employees have their reasons why they either choose to stay with their company for so long or join with another organization for a short period. They further stated that aside from the compensation and benefits, the company should consider good communication as another focus for the employee to stay until his tenure ends.

The best example of this position is the military personnel working in the government, where most of them retire at the age of 56. We can see the loyalty of these people, unlike the private staff where we have all the opportunities to switch to another company if the need arises. Therefore, president if he has his trust in the military generals because of their attributes and their trustworthy, loyalty, and commitment to their services they are appointed.

Back to compensation and benefits, its relative importance will vary following the individual's specific need. A bachelor or single employee will have a lower advantage as compared to those who are married. With the increasing cost of living in any economies, the married person needs more remuneration as compared to a single or bachelor employee. For those employees who are reaching forty and above, the employee retention program should be given due consideration by the company through the employment of benefit plans that cover health-related expenses and other elderly care. For younger employees, educational plans subsidies or tuition rebates would be more effective (Lochhead & Stephens, 2004).

Maccoby (1984) in his article, identified the job satisfaction of employees and supervisors of Bell System over five years and found that both employees were satisfied with their pay and benefits and were also motivated to work productively. This kind of situation in any organization can be considered as basic needs because remuneration and motivation are factors that go hand-in-hand without prejudice. However, if the company is not considerate and look at their position selflessly, then the reverse is true. Motivation cannot anymore be the yardstick of employee's esteem needs (4th Maslow's five hierarchical needs) or the 2nd element which is psychological needs.

Companies are directly challenged when creating a compensation structure that supports an employee development program. Some organizations are basing their pay raises on performance appraisal; unfortunately, most of them if not all fail to satisfy the employee's needs. Some organizations are conducting the team environment concept based on this research but when rewarding their employees most of the companies did it individually (Feldman, 2000). Employees sometimes were caught in the trap due to these inconsistencies. Eventually, this situation can cause frustration and demotivation by employees. It is ironic to see employees not provided their pay raises, yet their managers and top people in the organization are receiving their monthly rewards and perks (Feldman, 2000)

It is the company's mission to put their employees into the culture of employee development. One good example is Sears who created a new compensation system when they got into the business of employee development. Their first pay increment was used to offer pay increases to employees who were promoted, but they changed their policy for a system where their employees are provided a salary increase for lateral moves that are appropriate for their position (O'Herron and Simonsen, 1995). This kind of lateral incremental approach made the people happy for Sears.

No matter how hard the company will try to be generous, there is no guarantee will the employees keep their positions but might be looking for opportunities somewhere else. Dy (2015) in her research study shows that compensation alone, cannot keep the employee working for the company for a long time. When an employee is financially challenged and found some job elsewhere, he will gladly say to his/her employer, "Thank you and more power to you and your company. Because opportunity only knocks once, the offer from the other company must be accepted for greener pasture.

14. Recognition and Awards

An effective retention strategy for employees at any age is to provide skill recognition of personal job accomplishments (Yazinski, 2009). This author's hypothesis points out that the psychological needs and esteem needs relate to the employee's motivational element that missing this process can endanger the employee's allegiance to the company. Further,

Redington, (2007) in his study reveals that acknowledging individual work accomplishments prolongs the employment of employees within the company he is working.

Yazinski (2009) show some trends of an increased number of job applicants seeking out for companies that encourage employee's input, growth, education, and teamwork, beyond the traditional compensation/benefit. This study shows that any employee will be worth his salt. It means that any opportunity that may come their way, they will grab it due to employment security. The nature of a person is to live a better life through employment or having his own business. Recognition and rewards go hand-in-hand that Maslow's third hierarchical needs and second psychological needs to be appreciated with a pat on the back or a certificate of recognition or providing a plaque of appreciation in addition to the compensation and benefits to be rewarded simultaneously.

It shows that personal recognition is priceless in addition to the organizational benefits provided to an employee (The Gale Group, 2006). Moreover, basing from statistics the impact of verbal praise can enhance company loyalty, motivation, and perseverance at no extra charge. Redington (2007), emphasized that individual skill recognition is restricted by age, and motivates positive behavior, ethics, teamwork, confidence, and growth in all employees. Agrela et al., (2008) concluded that both skill recognition (ranging from verbal praise to incentives/rewards) and learning opportunities (growth/development) could enhance the individual's performance, effectiveness, and retention from the company he is employed.

15. Synthesis of the Study

The readings and reviews of all the literature and studies cited in this research work provide the impact that without these cited articles, research works, and journal among others, the research work cannot come up with a conceptual framework which is necessary for the researcher to have her research paradigm.

The citations were based on the demographic profiles and the strategic success factors based on the models provided by Agyeman and Ponniah (2014) Figure 1.1 Model and Maslow's Five Hierarchical Theory Figure 1.2, respectively. The researcher came up with theoretical framework employing the graphical workflow of the demographic profiles of both respondents, e.g., (1) age, (2) gender, (3) tenure, (4) education, and (5) income level in relation to the four human resource management practices such as (1) increasing job satisfaction, (2) providing good working environment, (3) career development opportunities, and (4) increasing recognition and rewards as shown in Figure 1.1, chapter 1.

In Figure 1.2, page 15, representing the Maslow's Theory on Five Hierarchy of Needs, shows the three foundational elements like the (1) Basic needs, (2) Psychological needs, and the (3) Self-fulfillment needs. These three fundamental elements contain five levels such as (a) physiological needs that consider food, water, warmth, and rest; (b) safety needs for security and safety; both (a) and (b) considered as basic needs (1); (c) belongingness and love needs as for intimate relationships and friends; (d) esteem needs for prestige and feeling of accomplishment; both (c) and (d) considered as psychological needs (2); (e) self-actualization in achieving one's full potential, including creative activities considered as self-fulfillment needs (3).

In summary, the five hierarchical needs of Maslow can be conducted into three elements like the basic, psychological, and self-fulfillment needs.

Figure 1.3, page 16 came out as the researcher's model basing from the two above-cited models.

The input variables which are the independent ones will now be represented by the (A) demographic profiles consisting of the elements such as the (1) age, (2) gender, (3) marital status, (4) highest educational attainment, (5) position, (6) hotel classification, and (7) service years in the company. Another input-independent variables are the (B) strategic success factors namely, (1) recruitment and selection, (2) compensation and benefits, (3) working environment and company culture, (4) job design and work teams, (5) career development and training, (6) performance management and evaluation, and (7) communications, and (8) rewards and recognition. The (B), (C), (E), (F), & (G) factors are also presented, Figure 1.3.

The graphical workflows (Figure 1.3) are shown with the researcher assessing the respondents' demographic profiles (A) as to their level of influence and importance of the retention factors let alone the managers' perceptions (C) as to their roles in the retention management of rank-and-file employees (B). It also shows if there will be significant differences between the respondents' assessments (D) on the level of influence and importance of the given eight retention management factors.

As the retention management factors (E) will be assessed as to their level of influence and level of importance using the statistical tool, it will then reveal the role of managers (F) in the retention management of rank-and-file employees.

The process workflow made the difference in the role of the managers in the retention of management of the rank-and-file employees after both the former and the later had perceived the significant relationship between the demographic profiles and strategic success factors which the readers can see the flow in Figure 1.3.

The graphical workflow further relates the managers' perception (C) and rank-and-file employees' perceptions (B) in the relationship between the demographic profiles (A) and the retention management strategic success factors (D) as detailed in Figure 1.3. It also shows the perceived level of influence and level of importance on retention management (E) in which the roles of the managers (F) will play a significance in the process. At the end of the workflow is the feedback (G) from both the retention manager and the rank-and-file employees.

Figure 1.4 presents the researcher's paradigm which is the input-process-output. The input is represented by the independent variables like the demographic profiles (A) and the strategic success factors (A). The process employs the identification, structured survey questionnaire, statistical tools and analyzed data, findings, and results (B) and (C). The output shows the role of the managers (D) in the retention management of rank-and-file employees (E). The feedback (F) will then be monitored and action to be taken by the retention managers (G).

The citations of studies, articles, journals, and other literature are based on the independent and dependent variables as provided in the statement of the problem as well as in the survey questionnaire to be consistent throughout the research study.

CHAPTER III

RESEARCH METHODOLOGY

This chapter explains the overall methodology to be used to collect the data and address the research issues. The selection and justification of the methods used should be considered first, and the structured survey questionnaire that provides information about the sample population in the selected hotels in Abu Dhabi follows. The instrument is described and defined including the data collection processes and the type of analysis carried out in this research.

1. Research Design

This research study used the descriptive-correlational research which deals mainly on a survey questionnaire. Penwarden (2014) defined a descriptive method of research as one that gathers quantifiable information that can be used for statistical inference on the target respondents through data analysis. This type of research was used to examine the current phenomenon that happens within Abu Dhabi's hotel industry. Through observations and descriptions of the background and profiles of respondents and their perceptions of the eight factors of employee retention, the researcher came up with this research design. The eight factors used throughout this study comprises of compensation and benefits, rewards and recognition, work environment and culture, recruitment and selection, career development and training, job design and work teams, performance and management evaluation, and communications.

Correlation analysis is also used in this study to measure the selected variables of interest. Correlation analysis as defined by Dudovskiy (2018) is used to understand the nature of relationships between two individual variables. It is used to analyze the relationship between a profile of the respondents and their perceptions on the level of influence and level of importance of the factors of employee retention, and the difference between the perception of managers and rank-and-file employees on the level of importance and level of influence of the factors of employee retention.

2. Researcher's Sources of Data

The initial list of hotels from Abu Dhabi comes from Trivago list (Retrieved from www.trivago.ae/Hotels/Abu Dhabi.) From this list, respondents are chosen from each hotel category, like a 5-Star hotel, 4-Star hotel, and 3-Star hotel. The respondents consist of the managers, and rank-and-file employees are selected from these respondent hotels within Abu Dhabi.

Assessment in the profiling of the respondents and the level of influence and importance of the retention factors through a structured survey questionnaire initially constructed by the researcher were conducted.

3. Sampling Design

Two hundred fifty (250) employees were chosen from the selected hotels and hotel apartments in Abu Dhabi grouped into two position levels: managers at 47 and rank-and-file at 203 employees. The total respondents were taken from the 5-Star hotel at one hundred sixteen (116), ninety-eight (98) from 4-Star hotels, and thirty-six (36) from 3-Star hotels.

Purposive probability sampling technique is used in determining the sample size out of the total population of managers and rank-and-file employees. Though the HR officers and department heads have picked them, a degree of control has been attributed to the researcher. The data is shown in Table 3.1.

Table 3.1. Distribution of Respondents

Employees	Hotels			Total	Percentage
	5-Star	4-Star	3-Star		
Manager	21	20	6	47	18.80
Rank-and-File	95	78	30	203	81.20
Total	116	98	36	250	100.00

4. Research Instrument

The researcher initially constructs the employee retention survey questionnaire which is used to gather data. The first part is used to measure the demographic profiles of the respondents while the second part measures the level of importance and level of influence of the retention factors taken from the eight success factors.

The survey questionnaire is designed with two main columns to determine the level of influence and level of importance on the factors of employee retention. The level of influence is the capacity of the factors to impact the employee's behavior and judgment in staying with the company. The level of importance is the factor having great significance and value to the employee to remain with the company.

The internal consistency and reliability of the instrument are measured using Cronbach alpha administered to 30 sample respondents. The content validity is assessed by three experts directly and engaged in hospitality management. (Retrieved from https://www.statisticshowto. Datascience central.com/ Cronbach's-alpha-spss/)

In order to determine and measure the level of influence and level of importance of the retention factors (compensation and benefits, rewards and recognition, work environment and culture, recruitment and selection, career development and training, job design and work teams, performance evaluation, and communications) based on the perceptions of the respondents, the Likert scale below is used.

Table 3.2. Likert Scale

Scale	Statistical Range	Interpretation	Level
5	4.21 – 5.00	Very Satisfied (VS)	Very High
4	3.41 – 4.20	Satisfied (SA)	High
3	2.61 – 3.40	Average (AV)	Average
2	1.81 – 2.60	Dissatisfied (DI)	Low
1	1.00 – 1.80	Very Dissatisfied (VD)	Very Low

5. Data Gathering Procedure

In this section, some ethical considerations must be conducted by the researcher. The first move was to prepare for the survey questionnaire using the demographic profiles and the success factors as mentioned in the research instrument. If the survey questionnaire is not original but copied from the existing and used questions by other researcher and it so happens that the same type of questions applies to the researcher's current study, the researcher should ask permission with the approval from her dean to use the same. It will provide the researcher with peace of mind likewise the original author of the personal patent and right. If approved, then the researcher will continue using the questionnaire. If the researcher prepares the researcher's questionnaire, then there is no need to write a request.

The next ethical move is to write a request to the hotel respondents about the researcher's intention with the approval from the university dean. After clearance on this concern, another application is to be sent to the same hotels, this time asking their support for their managers and rank-and-file employees to participate in the survey process. The ethical clearance through a letter of request will be addressed to human resource managers or department heads to grant permission in conducting this study in their hotel. The message of the application contains a confidentiality agreement and that a copy of the results from the survey will be given to the company for their further use. The said officers then distribute the survey questionnaire to the target respondents, e.g., managers and rank-and-file employees. An appointed date and time are set for the questionnaires to be answered.

The researcher made a personal appearance to the hotel HR officers and the department heads before the survey questionnaire is being distributed to ensure that the respondents know what to do in the conduct of the survey. The purpose of the survey will be briefly discussed to the respondents including the necessity of giving accurate and honest answers or responses, confidentiality of the results, and integrity of the given data for the success of the study.

After the commencement of the set date to answer, the survey questionnaires are retrieved by the researcher. Those that are correctly answered or responded have been considered and simplified in a matrix to maintain the accuracy of gathered data. Those with incomplete details or responses, mutilated and marked by the respondents with unnecessary and irrelevant comments are rejected and disregarded.

6. Statistical Treatment of Data

6.1. Frequency Count (f) and Percentage (%)

By using frequency distribution, an organized tabulation of data is categorized on the scale of measurement and the scores are systematically shown on an attribute or a measure to reflect how frequently each value is obtained. Scores obtained in frequency distribution are further measured using percentage. The frequency count and percentage are used to measure the independent variables enumerated explicitly in the profile of the respondents.

6.2. Arithmetic Mean ($\bar{x}$)

Statistical mean is used in this study to determine the average or the calculated central value of the given scores. For the set of data, the arithmetic mean is the mathematical expectation or the central value of a discrete set of numbers: some of the values divided by the number of items in the sample. The perception of the respondents on the level of influence and level of importance of retention factors are measured using the mean scores obtained in each factor by the total respondents of this present study.

6.3. Pearson Product Moment of Correlation (rxy)

Pearson Product Moment of Correlation or Pearson r is a powerful parametric statistical tool that measures the degree of linear relationship between variables. Just like the other correlation statistics, the correlation coefficient (r) determines the direction of the relationship (directly proportional or inversely proportional) and the strength of the relationship (stronger if closer to 1). This study measures the significant relationship between the profile of the respondents and their perception of the level of importance and level of influence of the retention factors. (Retrieved from

https://study.com/.../pearson-correlation-formula-example-significance.html.)

6.4. t-Test (t)

Measurement of the difference in mean scores of the two groups of respondents on the level of influence and level of importance of retention factors is conducted using t-Test of difference for independent samples. Since the difference cannot be determined as to its significance, it is further measured using t-Test of significance and to test the null hypothesis. (Retrieved from https:// www. statistics howto. datasciencecentral.com/probability-and-statistics-test).

6.5. The Use of Regression Analysis

The use of this statistical tool is for the testing the null hypothesis on the differences of the respondents' perceptions on the level of influence and level of importance of the eight success factors.

CHAPTER IV

RESULTS AND DISCUSSIONS

This section will show the results of the survey and discusses each question. As explained in chapter 1, this study aims to assess of the role of the manager in the retention management of the rank-and-file employees in regards to the level of influence and level of importance of the success factors of selected major hotels operating in Abu Dhabi of the United Arab Emirates.

1. The Extent of the Respondents' Demographic Profiles

1.1. Age Profile (Table 4.1)

There were about 250 respondents chosen by the researcher to participate in this research study. Out of the 250 respondents, about 67 percent comprises the lower age from 18 to 39 years old equivalent to 166. There was 25 percent consisting of the age of 40 to 49 years old equivalent to 63. The remaining 21 respondents were composed of 50 years old and above at 8 percent. Table 4.1 below presents the breakdown. The table further shows that 67 percent of the respondents are rank-and-file employees while the remaining 34 percent are on the manager positions.

Table 4.1 Age Profile

Age Bracket	Frequency	Percentage
60 and Above	3	1.10
50 – 59 years	18	7.20
40 – 49 years	63	25.20
30 – 39 years	113	45.30
18 – 29 years	53	21.20
Total	250	100.00

1.2. Gender Profile (Table 4.2)

The gender profile as shown in Table 4.2 indicates 147 males of the respondents at 59 percent. The remaining 103 respondents at 41 percent represent the female. It shows that more male employees were hired than their female counterpart at 59 percent by the hotel establishments of Abu Dhabi to perform the rank-and-file routine activities.

Table 4.2 Gender Profile

Gender	Frequency	Percentage
Male	147	58.80
Female	103	41.20
Total	250	100.00

1.3. Marital Status Profile (Table 4.3)

The marital status profile as shown in Table 4.3 reveals 55 percent married employees in different hotels of Abu Dhabi equivalent to 137. The next type of employees hired by the hotel industry is single at 32 percent or 81 respondents. Single parents and widowed respondents are recorded at 32 or 13 percent. It is inferred that most of those respondents who are engaged in the hotel industry are married people and holds on to their posts for survival. Conversely, the single and widowed respondents might be greener pasture opportunist when there are chances to grab any vacant positions in other industries.

Table 4.3. Marital Status Profile

Marital Status	Frequency	Percentage
Single	81	32.40
Single Parent	24	9.60
Married	137	54.80
Widowed	8	3.20
Total	**250**	**100.00**

1.4. Highest Educational Attainment Profile (Table 4.4)

Sixty percent of the respondents as shown in Table 4.4 are college graduates with some of them occupy the rank-and-file position. This profile was followed by master's degree holders at 20 percent holding the rank of manager position. The doctorate degrees represent 3 percent holding also the manager position. The college undergraduate represents

17 percent which is represented by the rank-and-file employees. It is also inferred that the hotel industry in Abu Dhabi possesses different educational qualifications suited in their respective positions.

Table 4.4. **Highest Educational Attainment Profile**

Education	Frequency	Percentage
Doctorate Degree	8	3.20
Master's Degree	51	20.40
College Graduate	150	60.00
College Undergraduate	41	16.40
Total	**250**	**100.00**

1.5. Position Profile (Table 4.5)

The below table 4.5, shows a more significant majority of the respondents are holding the rank-and-file level at 81 percent. The remaining respondents are the managers recorded at 19 percent. It is inferred that in the hotel industry about 19 percent are managing the activities such as the front desk, concierge, food, and beverages, room accommodations, maintenance, health and safety, restaurants, SPA, transportation, kitchen, administration office, accounting, HRM, and parking area among others. The rank-and-file are assigned to each unit or department to assist the managers in their daily tasks to attain the hotel's vision and mission and the specific objective.

Table 4.5. Position Profile

Position	Frequency	Percentage
Manager	47	18.80
Rank-and-File	203	81.20
Total	250	100.00

1.6. Hotel Classification Level (Table 4.6)

About 47 percent of the respondents working in the hotel establishment or 116 employees are hired by the 5-Star hotels (Table 4.6). The 4-Star hotels are frequented at 98 employees representing 39 percent. The 3-Star hotels are registered at 36 respondents with an equivalent 14 percent. This study is limited only to these three kinds of hotel. It is inferred that Abu Dhabi is providing their tourist guests with a better brand of hotels as represented by the 4-Star and 5-Star at 86 percent.

Table 4.6. Hotel Classification Level

Classification	Frequency	Percentage
5-Star	116	46.50
4-Star	98	39.10
3-Star	36	14.40
Total	250	100.00

1.7. Respondents' Years of Service in the Company (Table 4.7)

About 66 percent of the respondents are serving the hotel industry at the age of 5 years and below (Table 4.7). The table also shows that 34 percent are providing their services in the hotel establishments for over 5.1 years. It is inferred that some of this majority of respondents are not keen to work above eight years but quit if there is an opportunity for them to transfer maybe to another hotel which is new or having a good management environment. Further, there are fast turn-over of employees in the hotel industry as it demands younger human resources concerning the nature of the hospitality industry.

Table 4.7 Respondents' Years of Service in the Company

Years of Service	Frequency	Percentage
Over 8 years	27	10.80
5.1 – 8 years	57	22.80
2.1 – 5 years	95	38.00
2 years and below	71	28.40
Total	250	100.00

2. Respondents' Assessment in the Hotel Industry's Managers and Rank-and-file Employees through the Retention Management's Success Factors

2.1 On Level of Influence (Table 4.8)

Table 4.8 On Level of Influence as Perceived by Managers and Rank-and-File Employees of Retention Management's Success Factors

Retention Factors on Level of Influence	MP		R&FP		Both LOI		Action Plan
	Mgr	Rank	R&F	Rank	Ave	Rank*	
1. Compensation and Benefits	3.65	4	4.07	1	4	1	HL/DL
2. Work Environment and Corp. Culture	3.74	1	3.91	3	3.88	2	HL/DL
3. Communication	3.57	6	3.93	2	3.86	3	HL/DL
4. Performance Management and Eval.	3.7	2	3.87	4	3.84	4	HL/DL
5. Recognition and Rewards	3.62	5	3.87	5	3.82	5	HL/DL
6. Career Development and Training	3.53	7	3.85	6	3.79	6	HL/DL
7. Job Design and Work Teams	3.66	3	3.8	7	3.77	7	HL/DL
8. Recruitment and Selection	3.53	8	3.76	8	3.72	8	HL/DL
Overall	3.63		3.88		3.84		HL/DL

Note:

*Ranking is based on average mean between the Manager and the Rank-and-file.

MP = Managers' perception; R&FP = Rank & File perception; Both LOI = Both level of Influence.

HL/DL = High level/Doing less innovativeness.

Scale	Range	Interpretation	Level	Action Plan
5	4.21-5.00	Very Satisfied (VS)	Very High	Doing nothing
4	3.41-4.20	Satisfied (S)	High	Doing less
3	2.61-3.40	Average (A)	Average	Doing more
2	1.81-2.60	Dissatisfied (DS)	Low	Doing much more
1	1.00-1.80	Very Dissatisfied (VD)	Very Low	Total Enhancement

2.1.1. On the Level of Influence as perceived by the Managers (Table 4.8 Column 2 & 3)

Table 4.8 shows the managers' perceptions on the level of influence with work environment and corporate culture as (Rank 1), performance management and evaluation as (Rank 2), job design and work teams as (Rank 3), compensation and benefits as (Rank 4), recognition and rewards as (Rank 5), communication as (Rank 6), career development and training as (Rank 7), and recruitment and selection as (Rank 8).

2.1.2. On the Level of Influence as perceived by the Rank-and-file (Table 4.8 Col 4 & 5)

The rank-and-file perceptions show compensation and benefit as (Rank 1), communication as (Rank 2), work environment and corporate culture as (Rank 3), performance management and evaluation as (Rank 4), recognition and rewards as (Rank 5), career development and training as (Rank 6), Job design and work teams as (Rank 7), and recruitment and selection as (Rank 8).

The top three success factors as perceived by both respondents show compensation and benefits as (Rank 1), work environment and corporate culture as (Rank 2), and communication as (Rank 3).

2.1.3. Average on the Level of Influence as perceived by both Respondents (Table 4.8 Column 6 & 7)

Table 4.8 shows the average level of influence of retention management's success factors which comprises (Rank 1) for compensation and benefits, (Rank 2) for work environment and corporate culture,

(Rank 3) for communication, (Rank 4) for performance management and evaluation, (Rank 5) for recognition and rewards, (Rank 6) for career development and training, (Rank 7) for job design and work teams, and (Rank 8) for recruitment and selection in that order.

2.1.4. Assessment of the Level of Influence on Each Success Factor

(1) Compensation and benefits. The managers rated it at 3.65 mean, and the rank-and-file at 4.07 mean with a deviation of 0.42 a big gap in the assessment of the managers and the rank-and-file. It shows an average mean of 4.0 and rank as no. 1 with the same satisfaction, high level and doing less as the result of the finding. This factor is considered as the highest level of influence. It is inferred that most of the rank-and-file employees are considering this factor very important since it will provide them the day-to-day sustenance. Maslow's five hierarchical needs point out to this theory. Accordingly, it says that compensation is a yardstick of a person's struggle for a decent life. When applying for a job in any corporate organization either public or government, the person's line of focus is on the total remuneration he/she can place in his/her pocket every month. Although sometimes we will not be aware of this matter-of-factly situation, it is the human instinct that put a person in such a desperate position (Lochhead and Stephens, 2004). The authors further opined that there are facts to suggest when talking about compensation and benefits. These employees have their reasons why they either choose to stay with their company for so long or join with another organization for a short period. Its relative importance will vary following the individual's specific need. A bachelor or single employee will have a lower benefit as compared to those who are married. With

the increasing cost of living in any economies, the married person needs more remuneration as compared to a single or bachelor employee. For those employees who are reaching forty and above, the employee retention program should be given due consideration by the company through the employment of benefit plans that cover health-related expenses and other elderly care. For younger employees, educational plans subsidies or tuition rebates would be more effective (Lochhead & Stephens, 2004).

(2) Work environment and corporate culture. This factor was ranked as no. 2. The managers assessed it at 3.74 categorized as high. The rank-and-file assessed it at 3.91 categorized as high also at 0.17 standard deviation. Their average mean shows a 3.88 categorized as high with less to do in the enhancement of the factor. Deery (2008) in her study focused on the work-life balance where job attitudes are necessary for the employees to endure in their workplace through job satisfaction and their organizational commitment. These job attitudes, as well as their attributes like positive and negative affectivity, the role of work-life balance (WLB) and their employee turnover, need strategies to alleviate high turnover rates. The author recommends the need for legislation on maximum, as well as minimum working hours, good role models at the workplace, flexible working hours and arrangements, sound recruitment and training opportunities and company family-friendly work policies which can take effect on the work environment and corporate culture.

(3) Communication. This factor is considered as the no. three among the eight success factors as assessed by the respondents. The result shows the managers' assessment at 3.57 categorized as high. The rank-and-file assessed it at 3.93 classified as high also with a standard deviation of 0.36. Their average mean shows a 3.86 categorized as high with less to do in the enhancement of the factor. Cohn (2007) in his article pointed

out that effective communication requires paying attention to an entire process, not just the content of the message. When you are the messenger in this process, you should consider potential barriers at several stages that can keep your intended audience from receiving your signal. Be aware of how your attitudes, emotions, knowledge, and credibility with the receiver might impede or alter whether and how your message is received. Be mindful of your body language when speaking. Consider the attitudes and knowledge of your intended audience as well. Diversity in age, sex, and ethnicity or race add to the communication challenges, as do different training backgrounds. Individuals from different cultures may assign very different meanings to facial expressions, use of space, and, especially, gestures. For example, in some Asian cultures, women learn that it is disrespectful to look people in the eye and so they tend to have downcast eyes during a conversation. But in the United States, this body language could be misinterpreted as a lack of interest or a lack of attention.

(4) Performance management and evaluation. This factor is considered as the no. 4 among the eight success factors as assessed by the respondents. The result shows the managers' assessment at 3.70 categorized as high. The rank-and-file assessed it at 3.87 categorized as high also with a standard deviation of 0.17. Their average mean shows a 3.84 categorized as high with less to do in the enhancement of the factor. Osmania et al. (2012) in their article surmised that an organization's human resources are of great importance to its success. Without effective employees, organizations would work so ineffective and would risk failing to enforce claims of its objectives and mission. Therefore, every organization within the strategy that has, it applies the most appropriate system of performance management, a process

that helps in the commitment of all employees towards achieving the objectives of the organization.

Further in their study, if employees see that they are evaluated with their work and commitment, then this will result to motivate them to work harder. As a component related to performance evaluation, it would play an essential role in motivating employees. It will stimulate them as their salary will increase as well receive other forms of rewards such as appreciation/gratitude, praise, etc. Therefore, many international organizations or institutions within their organizational structure apply the method of the remuneration as a result of the excellent performance of their employees. The authors further stated that this kind of approach could be used elsewhere since the performance assessment process is seen as something more formal and must necessarily be accomplished by the leaders, where in most cases is done the subjective evaluation of left out without assessing the real capabilities and results of employee performance. The application of the method of remuneration as a result of the excellent performance of employees in public institutions can be a matter of choice because often-times the assessment is subjective and related to narrow personal or political according to management department or institution's political leaders. Also, an element that must be present in the evaluation of performance in other countries is to focus more attention on finding and application of methods for improving performance, rather than just their use without any positive result. It is suggested that in the future to organize workshops, conferences, roundtables and sessions aimed at different training and awareness of the reviewers of the importance of human resources, and the importance of assessing the value and contribution they provide that are propulsive towards a most successfully future of the organization or institution.

(5) Recognition and rewards. This factor as shown in the table was rated at 3.62 by the managers and 3.87 by the rank-and-file with an average mean of 3.82. It is ranked as no. Five as compared to the other factors. The result further shows that is has a high satisfaction with lesser to do in enhancing the factor. Although, as some employees will also consider that recognition and rewards could be a top priority while working in the hotel industry but the result shows otherwise. According to Yazinski (2009), an effective retention strategy for employees at any age is to provide skill recognition of personal job accomplishments. This author's hypothesis points out that the psychological needs and esteem needs relate to the employee's motivational element that missing this process can endanger the employee's allegiance to the company. Further, Redington, (2007) in his study reveals that acknowledging individual work accomplishments prolongs the employment of employees within the company he is working. Suffice to say; it is the author's viewpoint that recognition and rewards should be one of the top priorities in the retention of employees.

(6) Career development and training. This factor is considered as the no. 6 among the eight success factors as assessed by the respondents. The result shows the managers' assessment at 3.53 categorized as high. The rank-and-file assessed it at 3.85 categorized as high also with a standard deviation of 0.32. Their average mean shows a 3.79 categorized as high with less to do in the enhancement of the factor. Yahya and Go (2002) observed that in the development of employees, it should focus on achieving quality, creativity, leadership, and problem-solving skill. These development phases could be enhanced by way of training, decision-making, performance appraisal, and compensation and reward. An employee being developed in his career should cope with knowledge management like knowledge acquisition, knowledge documentation,

knowledge transfer, knowledge creation, and knowledge application. The authors further opined that combining these two approaches like the development and training of employees through knowledge management would mean some benefits that the company can get from the employees.

(7) Job design and work teams. This factor is considered as the no. Seven among the eight success factors as assessed by the respondents. The result shows the managers' assessment at 3.66 categorized as high. The rank-and-file assessed it at 3.80 categorized as high also with a standard deviation of 0.14. Their average mean shows a 3.77 categorized as high with less to do in the enhancement of the factor. Daniels et al. (2017) in their study investigated the role of other employment practices, either as instruments for job redesign or as instruments that augment job redesign. It focused on the employee's well-being considering performance as an outcome by reviewing thirty-three intervention studies. The author's finding shows that well-being and performance may be improved by training workers in enhancing their jobs, redesign the job, and wide approaches to the existing system by way of enhancing job design and a range of other employment practices. The author concluded that successful implementation of interventions should be associated with worker involvement and engagement, managerial commitment and integration with other organizational systems. McEwan et al. (2017) conducted a systematic review and meta-analysis of teamwork interventions using a controlled experimental design by way of literature search returned 16,849 unique articles to improve teamwork and team performance. They concluded that Interventions appear to be particularly effective when they target multiple dimensions of teamwork and include experiential activities for team members to learn about, practice actively, and continually develop teamwork.

(8) Recruitment and selection. This factor is considered as the last to be on the top priority since it was assessed as no. 8. The result shows the managers' assessment at 3.53 categorized as high. The rank-and-file assessed it at 3.76 categorized as high also with a standard deviation of 0.23. Their average mean shows a 3.72 categorized as high with less to do in the enhancement of the factor. Wright and McMahan (1992) observed that the use of human capital must have an implementing guide for the corporate organization to sustain and operate within a period. The authors further opined that such policy needs a fundamental characteristic for having a fit. It means the utilization of human resources to help achieve the organization goals. Schuler and Jackson (1987) collaborated this finding by saying that the fit involves the alignment of human resource management policies and practices and the organization's other functional strategies which was viewed as a critical step towards ultimate corporate goal achievement. Two more authors (Baird and Meshoulam, 1988), and (Wei, 2006) defined it by implying alignment and congruence among the various HRM practices and identifying it as systems, processes, and rewards respectively. It is inferred as a matter of HRM practices, that recruitment and selection, should be done right the first time to avoid a negative impact in the corporate implementation of goals and objectives.

2.2. On Level of Importance of Retention Management's Success Factors (Table 4.9)

The level of importance of retention management's success factors as presented in Table 4.9 comprises the eight success factors. These include communication, performance management and evaluation, work environment and corporate culture, compensation and benefits, career development and training, job design and work teams, recruitment and selection, recognition and rewards in that order as assessed by the respondents. The factors mentioned above are the basis of the managers and the rank-and-file in the assessment of the employees of the selected hotel establishments in the city of Abu Dhabi. The result shows the level of importance in retaining their employment.

Table 4.9 Retention Management's Success Factors on Level of Importance

Retention Factors On Level of Importance	X1 Mgr	X2 R&F	Y1 Ave	Cat	Level	Rank*	Action Plan
1. Communication	3.89	4.06	4.03	S	H	1	Doing less
2. Performance Management and Eval.	3.83	4.03	4	S	H	2	Doing less
3. Work Environment and Corp. Culture	3.81	4.02	3.98	S	H	3	Doing less
4. Compensation and Benefits	3.66	4.08	3.96	S	H	4	Doing less
5. Career Development and Training	3.79	3.97	3.94	S	H	5	Doing less
6. Job Design and Work Teams	3.64	4	3.94	S	H	6	Doing less
7. Recruitment and Selection	3.87	3.94	3.93	S	H	7	Doing less
8. Recognition and Rewards	3.66	3.95	3.9	S	H	8	Doing less
Overall	3.77	4.01	3.96	S	H		Doing less

*Ranking is based on average mean between the Manager and the Rank-and-file

Scale	Range	Interpretation	Level	Action Plan
5	4.21-5.00	Very Satisfied (VS)	Very High	Doing nothing
4	3.41-4.20	Satisfied (S)	High	Doing less
3	2.61-3.40	Average (A)	Average	Doing more
2	1.81-2.60	Dissatisfied (DS)	Low	Doing much more
1	1.00-1.80	Very Dissatisfied (VD)	Very Low	Total Enhancement

2.2.1. Level of Importance on Each Success Factor (Table 4.9)

(1) Communication. The managers rated it at 3.89 mean, and the rank-and-file at 4.06 mean with a deviation of 0.17 a medium gap in the assessment of the respondents. It showed an average mean of 4.03 and ranked as no. 1 with the same satisfaction, high level and doing less as the result of the finding. This factor is considered as the 1st level of importance. Communication in a workplace is essential especially in the diverse workplace where mixed nationalities are working in the hotel establishments. Guests coming from different countries need people who are diverse as well in verbal communication.

(2) Performance management and evaluation. The managers rated it at 3.83 mean, and the rank-and-file at 4.03 mean with a deviation of 0.20 a medium gap in the assessment of the respondents. It showed an average mean of 4.0 and ranked as no. 2 with the same satisfaction, high level and doing less as the result of the finding. This factor is considered as the 2nd level of importance. It is the researcher's opinion that this level should be next to the compensation and benefits because after an employee is recruited and operating performance will follow with a relative remuneration to provide motivation.

(3) Work environment and corporate culture. The managers rated it at 3.81 mean, and the rank-and-file at 4.02 mean with a deviation of 0.21 a medium gap in the assessment of the managers and the rank-and-file. It showed an average mean of 3.98 and ranked as no. 3 with the same satisfaction, high level and doing less as the result of the finding. This factor is considered as the 3rd level of importance. It is inferred that most of the rank-and-file employees are considering this factor less highly important since it will provide them only some kind of work convenience and the company's social responsibility to their employees.

(4) Compensation and benefits. The managers rated it at 3.66 mean, and the rank-and-file at 4.08 mean with a deviation of 0.42 a big gap in the assessment of the managers and the rank-and-file. It shows an average mean of 3.96 and rank as no. 4 with the same satisfaction, high level and doing less as the result of the finding. This factor is considered as the 4th level of importance. It is inferred that most of the rank-and-file employees are considering this factor highly important since it will provide them the day-to-day sustenance.

(5) Career development and training. The managers rated it at 3.79 mean, and the rank-and-file at 3.97 mean with a deviation of 0.18 a lesser medium gap in the assessment of the respondents. It showed an average mean of 3.94 and ranked as no. 5 with the same satisfaction, high level and doing less as the result of the finding. This factor is considered as the 5th level of importance. This researcher maintains that career development and training should be on the top five of the success factors because it can provide the employees some motivation especially if they are looking forward in working with the hotel industry on long-term base employment.

(6) Job design and work teams. The managers rated it at 3.64 mean, and the rank-and-file at 4 mean with a deviation of 0.36 a medium gap in the assessment of the respondents. It showed an average mean of 3.94 and ranked as no. 6 with the same satisfaction, high level and doing less as the result of the finding. This factor is considered as the 6th level of importance. Job design and work teams should always go hand-in-hand since the job and position will be relative to the team working environment in the areas of the hotel operations for delivering quality and best service to their guests.

(7) Recruitment and selection. The managers rated it at 3.87 mean, and the rank-and-file at 3.94 mean with a deviation of 0.07 a lesser

medium gap in the assessment of the managers and the rank-and-file. It showed an average mean of 3.93 and ranked as no. 7 with the same satisfaction, high level and doing less as the result of the finding. This factor is considered as the 7th level of importance. It is inferred that most of the employees are considering this factor less highly important since all of them have not affected anymore in the recruitment and selection process and are already in with the company. It should be noted here that this factor should be considered as number one when they as future employees underwent with this process. Remember that without an excellent recruitment and selection process conducted by the HRM unit, future employees that do not quality are recruited and employed would contribute to operational failure in the corporate's vision and mission statement.

(8) Recognition and rewards. The managers rated it at 3.66 mean, and the rank-and-file at 3.95 mean with a deviation of 0.29 a medium gap in the assessment of the managers and the rank-and-file. It shows an average mean of 3.90 and rank as no. 8 with the same satisfaction, high level and doing less as the result of the finding. This factor is considered as the 8th level of importance. It is inferred that most of the rank-and-file employees are considering this factor less highly important since it will provide them only some kind of recognition and probably a pat on the back and some small rewards as necessary.

2.2.2. Overall Level of Importance

It shows that the managers' responses were rated at 3.77 as mean categorized as satisfied at a high level and less action to be done. The rank-and-file shows a mean of 4.01. The average mean as reflected in the table shows 3.96 with a high level categorized as satisfied with less action on innovation. It means that the employees are contended with what they have now with the hotel industry on the level of importance.

2.3. On Level of Influence and Level of Importance of Retention Management's Success Factors (Table 4.10)

2.3.1. Overall Level of Influence and Level of Importance

Table 4.10 shows that the respondents' responses on the level of influence were rated at 3.84 as mean and the level of importance at 3.96 with an average mean of 3.90 categorized as satisfied at high level and less action to be done as presented in Table 4.10. It means that the employees are contended with what they have now with the hotel industry on the level of influence and importance.

Table 4.10 Retention Management's Success Factors on Level of Influence and Level of Importance

Retention Factors	X1	X2	Y1				
On Level of Influence and Importance	Inf	Imp	Ave	Cat	Level	Rank	Action Plan
Compensation and Benefits	4	3.96	3.98	S	H	1	Doing less
Communication	3.86	4.03	3.95	S	H	2	Doing less
Work Environment and Corporate Culture	3.88	3.98	3.93	S	H	3	Doing less
Performance Management and Evaluation	3.84	4	3.92	S	H	4	Doing less
Career Development and Training	3.79	3.94	3.87	S	H	5	Doing less
Job Design and Work Teams	3.77	3.94	3.86	S	H	6	Doing less
Recognition and Rewards	3.82	3.9	3.86	S	H	7	Doing less
Recruitment and Selection	3.72	3.93	3.83	S	H	8	Doing less
Overall	3.84	3.96	3.90	S	H		Doing less

Note: Influence (Inf), Importance (Imp), Average (Ave), Category (Cat)

Scale	Range	Interpretation	Level	Action Plan
5	4.21-5.00	Very Satisfied (VS)	Very High	Doing nothing
4	3.41-4.20	Satisfied (S)	High	Doing less
3	2.61-3.40	Average (A)	Average	Doing more
2	1.81-2.60	Dissatisfied (DS)	Low	Doing much more
1	1.00-1.80	Very Dissatisfied (VD)	Very Low	Total Enhancement

2.3.2. Level of Influence and Importance on Each Success Factor (Table 4.10)

(1) Compensation and benefits. The respondents rated it at 4.0 mean for level of influence and 3.96 mean for level of importance with a standard deviation of 0.04 a lesser gap. It shows an average mean of 3.98 and rank as no. 1 with the same satisfaction, high level and doing less as the result of the finding. This factor is considered as the 1st level of influence and importance. It is inferred that the respondents consist of the managers and the rank-and-file employees are considering this factor as the top priority since it will provide them the day-to-day sustenance.

(2) Communication. The respondents rated it at 3.86 mean for level of influence and 4.03 mean for level of importance with a standard deviation of 0.27 a medium gap. It shows an average mean of 3.95 and rank as no. 2 (from no. 8 originally) with the same satisfaction, high level and doing less as the result of the finding. This factor is considered as the second level of influence and importance. It is inferred that the respondents consist of the managers and the rank-and-file employees are considering this factor as the second top priority since it will provide them the day-to-day good working relationship with their colleagues in the hotel industry.

(3) Work environment and corporate culture. The respondents rated it at 3.88 mean for level of influence and 3.98 mean for level of importance with a standard deviation of 0.10 a lesser gap. It shows an average mean of 3.93 and maintain the rank as no. 3 (from no. 3 originally) with the same satisfaction, high level and doing less as the result of the finding. This factor is considered as the third level of influence and importance. It is inferred that the respondents consist of the managers and the rank-and-file employees are considering this factor as the third top priority since it will provide them the day-to-day good working environment and the corporate social responsibility in which the company provided to them as well as the community activities.

(4) Performance management and evaluation. The respondents rated it at 3.84 mean for level of influence and 4.0 mean for level of importance with a standard deviation of 0.16 a lesser gap. It shows an average mean of 3.92 and ranked as no. 4 (from no. 7 originally) with the same satisfaction, high level and doing less as the result of the finding. This factor is considered as the fourth level of influence and importance. It is inferred that the respondents consist of the managers and the rank-and-file employees are considering this factor as the fourth top priority because it will provide them the motivation after a hard days' work by receiving future better incentives through the performance appraisal at the end of each term or on a yearly work evaluation basis.

(5) Career development and training. The respondents rated it at 3.79 mean for level of influence and 3.94 mean for level of importance with a standard deviation of 0.15 a lesser gap. It shows an average mean of 3.87 and maintain the rank of no. 5 (from no. 5 originally) with the same satisfaction, high level and doing less as the result of the finding. This factor is considered as the fifth level of influence and importance.

It is inferred that the respondents consist of the managers and the rank-and-file employees are considering this factor as the fifth top priority because it will help them in their career on a long-run with the hotel industry.

(6) Job design and work teams. The respondents rated it at 3.77 mean for level of influence and 3.94 mean for level of importance with a standard deviation of 0.17 a lesser gap. It shows an average mean of 3.86 and maintain the rank of no. 6 (from no. 6 originally) with the same satisfaction, high level and doing less as the result of the finding. This factor is considered as the sixth level of influence and importance. It is inferred that the respondents consist of the managers and the rank-and-file employees are considering this factor as the sixth top priority because it will be consistent for the employees working in their designed job or position and working as a team for better quality and productivity either in short-term or long-term employment.

(7) Recognition and rewards. The respondents rated it at 3.82 mean for level of influence and 3.90 mean for level of importance with a standard deviation of 0.08 a lesser gap. It shows an average mean of 3.86 and ranked as no. 7 similar to job design and work teams (from no. 2 originally) with the same satisfaction, high level and doing less as the result of the finding. This factor is considered as the seventh level of influence and importance. It is inferred that the respondent employees are considering this factor as the sixth or seventh top priority because this success factor will be the resulting output for any sacrifices that they will do for the good and benefit of the hotel establishments. The employee will be recognized at the end of each year for the excellent work they have done to the organization thus it is expected that their hard labor will not be in vain.

(8) <u>Recruitment and selection</u>. The respondents rated it at 3.72 mean for level of influence and 3.93 mean for level of importance with a standard deviation of 0.21 a medium gap. It shows an average mean of 3.83 and ranked as no. 7 or 8 like recognition and rewards (from no. 4 originally) with the same satisfaction, high level and doing less as the result of the finding. This factor is considered as the eight level of influence and importance. It is inferred that the respondent employees are not considering this as a top priority factor because for them they are immaterial as existing employees. For new hotel establishments, it might be a different situation meaning it will be number one success factor to hire a qualified and excellent recruit.

3. Significant Relationship between the Demographic Profiles of the Respondents and the Level of Influence and Level of Importance of Retention Factors

The significant relationship between the demographic profiles of the respondents and their assessment on the level of influence and level of importance of the retention factors is measured and determined using Pearson Product Moment of Correlation (r_{xy}). Because the sample size is two hundred fifty (250), the strength of the relationship or correlation may be low but still significant. The value of the correlation coefficient determines the direction of the relationship. Thus, a negative coefficient shows an inversely proportional relationship while a positive value means that the relationship is directly proportional.

3.1. Significant Relationship between Respondents Profiles and their Perception on the Retention Factors on the Level of Influence

Table 4.11 Significant Relationship between Respondents Profiles and their Perception on the Retention Factors on the Level of Influence and Level of Importance

All Respondents Profiles	Retention Factors			
	Level of Influence		Level of Importance	
	rxy	sig.	rxy	sig.
1. Age	**0.1845**	**0.0108**	**0.6712**	**0.0000**
2. Gender	-0.0192	0.9561	-0.0173	0.9586
3. Marital Status	0.0411	0.5738	0.0411	0.5738
4. Highest Educational Attainment	**0.2886**	**0.0000**	**0.3323**	**0.0000**
5. Hotel Classification	**0.1941**	**0.0108**	**0.2093**	**0.0045**
6. Position	**0.1534**	**0.0480**	**0.1986**	**0.0107**
7. Years of Service	**0.2415**	**0.0006**	**0.1988**	**0.0107**

Table 4.11 shows the significant relationship between the demographic profiles of respondents and their perception of the retention factors regarding the level of influence as highlighted. The demographic profiles consider the age, gender, marital status, highest educational attainment, hotel classification, position, and years of service.

The level of influence shows the demographic profiles in bold namely, (1) Age (rxy=0.1845), and significance of 0.0108; (4) Highest Educational Attainment (rxy=0.2886), and significance at 0.0000; (5) Hotel Classification (rxy=0.1941), and significance at 0.0108; (6)

Position (rxy=0.1534) and significance at 0.0480; and (7) Years of Service (rxy=0.2415) and significance at 0.0006. The figures as presented in the table shows a significant relationship to the level of influence of retention factors. The positive correlation coefficients indicate that the relationship between the correlated variables is directly proportional. An increase in the independent variable necessarily means that the independent variable also increases, or both decreases at the same time. Thus, the level of influence is higher for those older compared to those younger respondents, or those with higher educational attainment assess the retention factors higher compared to those with lower educational attainment.

The same table shows that the computed coefficients of the five demographic profiles, such as age, highest educational attainment, hotel classification, position, and years of service are higher compared to their tabular or critical value (two-tailed) distribution, therefore the hypothesis is rejected. The statistical data shows, therefore, there is a significant relationship between demographic profiles (age, highest educational attainment, hotel classification, position and years of service) and level of influence of retention factors.

3.2. Significant Relationship between Respondents Profile and their Perceptions on the Retention Factors on Level of Importance

The above table (Table 4.11) shows the significant relationship between demographic profiles of respondents and their perception on the level of importance on the retention factors.

The table also shows the demographic profiles in bold namely, (1) Age (rxy=0.6712), and significance of 0.0000; (4) Highest Educational Attainment (rxy=0.3323), and significance at 0.0000; (5) Hotel

Classification (rxy=0.2093), and significance at 0.0045; (6) Position (rxy=0.1986) and significance at 0.0107; and (7) Years of Service (rxy=0.1988) and significance at 0.0107. The figures as presented in the table shows a significant relationship to the level of importance of retention factors. The positive correlation coefficients indicate that the relationship between the correlated variables is directly proportional. An increase in the independent variable necessarily means that the independent variable also increases, or both decreases at the same time. Thus, the level of influence is higher for those older compared to those younger respondents, or those with higher educational attainment assess the retention factors higher compared to those with lower educational attainment.

The variables are significantly related to the level of importance of retention factors because the computed correlation coefficients are higher compared to the critical or tabular values at significant levels not exceeding 0.05 in a 2-tailed distribution. Therefore, the hypothesis is rejected because there is a significant relationship between a profile (age, highest educational attainment, hotel classification, position and years of service) and level of importance of retention factors.

3.3. Marital Status and Level of Influence of Managers Profile

Table 4.12 Significant Relationship between Profile of Managers and their Perception on the Retention Factors

Managers Profile	Retention Factors			
	Level of Influence		Level of Importance	
	rxy	sig.	rxy	sig.
1. Age	-0.1576	0.3479	**0.6776**	**0.0000**

2. Gender	0.1603	0.2827	-0.0189	0.8999
3. Marital Status (Rejected)	**-0.3480**	**0.0194**	**-0.2087**	**0.1777**
4. Highest Educational Attainment	-0.0049	0.9800	-0.1024	0.5036
5. Hotel Classification	-0.1911	0.2260	-0.1071	0.5036
6. Years of Service	-0.1390	0.4217	0.0283	0.8938

Table 4.12 shows *marital status* ($rxy=-0.3480$) of managers is significantly related (0.0194) to the level of influence of retention factors. The negative correlation coefficient means that a high level of influence in one marital status suffices low level of influence with that of the others or vice versa. Since the computed correlation coefficient is greater than its tabular or critical value ($rxy=-0.3480 > p, 0.0194$), the hypothesis is rejected ($0.0194<0.05$ LOS) because *marital status* is significantly related to the level of influence (0.05) of retention factors.

3.4. Age Profile and Level of Importance of Managers Profile

The same table (Table 4.12) shows the *age* ($rxy=0.6776$) to be significantly related (0.0000) to the perceived level of importance of retention factors by managers. With the computed coefficient higher than its tabular or critical value ($rxy=0.6776 > p, 0.0000$), the hypothesis is rejected ($0.0000<0.05$ LOS). The result shows that the relationship between age of managers and their assessment on the level of importance of retention factors was significant.

3.5. Rank-and-File Profiles and Level of Influence

In Table 4.13, the data shows that the highest educational attainment (rxy=0.2822) with significance of 0.0000 and hotel classification (rxy=0.2197) with significance of 0.0045 are significantly related to the level of influence of retention factors. The data shows that they are greater than their tabular or critical values in a 2-tailed distribution table. Thus, the *__hypothesis is rejected__* because the highest educational attainment and hotel classification are significantly related to the level of influence of retention factors.

Table 4.13 Significant Relationship between Profile of Rank-and-File Employees and Their Perception on the Retention Factors

Rank-and-File Profiles	Retention Factors			
	Level of Influence		Level of Importance	
	rxy	sig.	rxy	sig.
1. Age	-0.0408	0.5739	-0.0470	0.5740
2. *Gender*	0.0976	0.2601	**0.1697**	**0.0236**
3. Marital Status	-0.0234	0.7786	-0.0261	0.7788
4. *Highest Educational Attainment*	**0.2822**	**0.0000**	**0.2707**	**0.0002**
5. *Hotel Classification*	**0.2197**	**0.0045**	**0.2363**	**0.0015**
6. *Years of Service*	-0.0889	0.2601	-0.1339	0.0485

3.6. Rank-and-File Profiles and Level of Importance

The same table (Table 4.13) revealed that the gender profile (rxy=0.1697), with a p of 0.0236; highest educational attainment (rxy=0.2707), with a p of 0.0002, hotel classification (rxy=0.2363) with a p of 0.0015; and years of service (rxy=-0.1339) with a p of 0.0485 are significantly related to the level of importance of retention factors. The negative correlation between years of service and level of importance shows that the longer the stay of an employee in the company, the lower the level of importance of retention factors, or vice versa. This correlation result because the established relationship between the profiles and the level of importance is inversely proportional.

The level of importance as revealed in the above table clearly defined the correlation coefficients on gender (rxy=0.1697 > p, 0.0236), highest educational attainment (rxy=0.2707 >p. 0.0002), hotel classification (rxy=0.2363 > p, 0.0015) and years of service (rxy=-0.1339 > p, 0.0485) to be greater than their tabular or critical value in a 2-tailed distribution. Therefore, the ***hypothesis is rejected***. A significant relationship exists between a profile (gender, highest educational attainment, hotel classification and years of service) and level of importance of retention factors as perceived by rank-and-file employees.

4. Significant Differences between the Assessments of the Respondents on the Influence and the Level of Importance of Retention Factors

The differences between the assessments of the two groups of respondents on the level of influence and level of importance are determined using t-Test of difference for samples with two different sample sizes, and the hypothesis is tested using t-Test for hypothesis testing. A summary table is presented which contains the sample size per group (n), a summation of mean scores (ΣX), a summation of squares of mean scores (ΣX^2), a sum of squares (SS), and overall mean score of each group (Mean). The data is further analyzed by computing the value of t and comparing it with its tabular or critical value based on the calculated degrees of freedom.

Table 4.14 Significant Difference in the Level of Influence of Retention Factors

	Rank-and-File(A)	Managers(B)	Total
n	203	47	250
ΣX	788.2600	170.3000	958.5600
ΣX^2	3187.1488	648.6718	3835.8206
S S	126.2925	31.6061	160.4715
Mean	3.8831	3.6234	3.8342
MeanA - MeanB	t	df	p
0.2596	2.01	248	0.045514 **
0.2316	1.95	66.75	0.027577 *

Legend: ** = 2-tailed distribution
* = 1-tailed distribution

4.1. On Level of Influence

Table 4.14 shows the significant difference in the level of influence of retention factors. On the first assumption that the two sample sizes have equal variances, the computed value of t is 2.01. It is revealed that t-computed is greater than t-tabular based on the value found at 248 degrees of freedom (t=2.01> p, 0.045514). The ___hypothesis is rejected___ because there is a significant difference between the perception of the managers and rank-and-file employees on the level of influence of retention factors.

The same is true on the second assumption that the two sample sizes have different variances, where the computed t (1.95) is greater than its tabular value at 66.75 degrees of freedom (t=1.95 > p, 0.027577). The hypothesis is likewise rejected because there is a significant difference between the perception of managers and rank-and-file employees on the level of influence of retention factors.

4.2. On Level of Importance

Table 4.15 Significant Difference in the Level of Importance of Retention Factors

	Rank-and-File (A)	Managers (B)	Total
n	203	47	250
Σ X	812.5400	177.2400	989.7800
Σ X²	3368.8352	694.2062	4063.0414
S S	116.5138	25.8228	144.3836
Mean	4.0027	3.7711	3.9591
MeanA - MeanB	t	df	p
0.2316	1.89	248	0.029962 *
0.2316	1.90	69.59	0.0304675 *

Legend: ** = 2-tailed distribution
        * = 1-tailed distribution

Table 4.15 shows the significant difference in the level of importance of retention factors. On the first assumption that the two sample sizes have equal variances, the computed t (1.89) is greater than its tabular value at 248 degrees of freedom (t=1.89 > p, 0.029962). The ***hypothesis is rejected*** because there is a significant difference between the assessment of managers and rank-and-file employees on the level of importance of retention factors.

On the second assumption that the two independent samples have unequal sample variances, the computed t value is greater than its tabular value at 69.59 degrees of freedom (t=1.90 > p, 0.0304675). It means that the hypothesis is rejected because there is a significant difference in the perceptions of the managers and rank-and-file employees on the level of importance of retention factors.

5. The role of managers in the retention management of rank-and-file employees

Managerial employees play a vital role in business operations and who are given trust and confidence different from those given to supervisory and rank-and-file employees. Their duties consist in the performance of work directly related to management policies of their employer and regularly exercise discretion and independent judgment. In Section 2, Rule I, Book Three of the Omnibus Rules, managerial employees is defined as one who meets the following qualifications: (1) The primary duty consists of the management of the establishment in which they are employed, or of a department or subdivision thereof; (2) They customarily and regularly direct the work of two or more employees therein; and (3) They have the duty to hire or fire employees of lower rank; or their suggestions and recommendations as to hiring and firing, and to the promotion or any other change of status of other employees, are given particular weight (Retrieved from https://

www.google.com/search?q=Section+2%2C+Rule+I%2C+Book+Three+of+the+Omnibus+Rules%2C)

Table 4.16 Role of Managers in Retention Management of Rank-and-File Employees

Retention Factors	Level of Influence	Level of Importance
Compensation and Benefits	3.65	3.66
Recognition and Rewards	3.62	3.66
Work Environment and Corporate Culture	**3.74 (1)**	3.81
Recruitment and Selection	3.53	**3.87 (2)**
Career Development and Training	3.53	3.79
Job Design and Work Teams	**3.66 (3)**	3.64
Performance Management and Evaluation	**3.70 (2)**	**3.83 (3)**
Communication	3.57	**3.89 (1)**

Note: Ranking are presented in 1, 2, & 3 under the level of influence and level of importance.

This study utilizes eight retention factors (Table 4.16) such as compensation and benefits, recognition and rewards, work environment and corporate culture, recruitment and selection, career development and training, job design and work teams, performance management and evaluation, and communication. The perception of the managers on the other factors as regards their level of influence and level of importance indicates their role in retention management of rank-and-file employees. As such, these are the factors that they consider in the retention of rank-and-file employees.

5.1. Level of Influence

On the level of influence (Table 4.16), it shows that the work environment and corporate culture (3.74) is assessed by managers to be the most influential. It supports the study of (Renah and Setyadi, 2014) that there was a significant effect between the working environment and working motivation. The activities like performance management and evaluation (3.70), and job design and work teams (3.66) complete the three most influential factors. It means that the retention of rank-and-file may be based on these three retention factors with the highest mean rating as such managers consider the three factors as strong level of influence in their decision-making on issues about rank-and-file retention.

5.2. Level of Importance

On the level of importance (Table 4.6), it shows communication (3.89) as the most important among all retention factors. The main reason is the expectation of a good communication skill in the hospitality industry. Miscommunications often end in undesirable effects. It may affect the business operation and may even prolong in several periods when the hotel clients are in diversity.

The respondent managers also consider recruitment and selection (3.87) as potent retention factor for rank-and-file. The reason for this assessment is that the screening of employees starts with the issue of recruitment and selection. At this stage, the employer can shortlist all the applicants and be able to identify the most qualified among them. On the first hand, when the organization needs to employ somebody, the recruitment process is necessary for this purpose by applying an application form. On the other hand, a selection is used in choosing from applicants a suitable candidate to fill a post. With this position, managers at all levels are expected to show responsibility and diligence in making their choice, including retention of rank-and-file employees.

Another important factor is performance management and evaluation (3.83). This factor reflects the overall performance of the employee reflected and measured quantitatively. The managers may revisit this factor in decision making affecting retention issues if they do not personally witness the actual performance of the rank-and-file employees. It is designed to measure how an employee effectively performs his/her assigned duties. According to Walker and Moore (2011), a manager has to use information which helps in identifying solutions to improve program operations by way of developing a better understanding of their program's strengths and challenges.

CHAPTER V

SUMMARY, CONCLUSION, AND RECOMMENDATIONS

This study aims to assess in the hotel industry's retention management of the rank-and-file employees in terms of the demographic profiles and the level of influence and level of importance of the success factors of selected major hotels operating in Abu Dhabi of the United Arab Emirates.

SUMMARY OF FINDINGS

Below are the salient features of the research study in terms of summary of findings.

1. The Extent of the Respondents' Demographic Profiles

1.1. Position Level. Eighty-one percent are rank-and-file level while the managers at 19 percent. It is inferred that in the hotel industry about 19 percent are managing the activities such as the front desk, concierge, food, and beverages, room accommodations, maintenance, health and safety, restaurants, SPA, transportation, kitchen, administration office, accounting, HRM, and parking area among others.

1.2. Highest Educational Attainment Profile. Sixty percent of the respondents are college graduates with some of them occupies the rank-and-file position, master's degree holders at 20 percent holding the rank of manager position, and 3 percent for the doctorate degrees holding also the manager position. The college undergraduate represents 17 percent which is represented by the rank-and-file employees. It is also inferred that the hotel industry in Abu Dhabi possesses different educational qualifications suited in their respective positions.

1.3. Age Profile. Sixty seven percent comprises the lower age from 18 to 39 years old, 25 percent for the age of 40 to 49 years old and 8 percent for 50 years old and above. About 67 percent of the respondents are rank-and-file employees while the remaining 34 percent are on the manager positions.

1.4. Gender Profile. Fifty-nine percent are males, and 41 percent represents the female. It shows that more male employees were hired than their female counterpart by the hotel establishments of Abu Dhabi to perform the rank-and-file routine activities.

1.5. Marital Status Profile. Fifty-five percent are married employees while single at 32 percent, single parents and widowed respondents are 13 percent. It is inferred that most of those respondents who are engaged in the hotel industry are married people and holds on to their posts for survival.

1.6. Years of Service in the Company. About 66 percent of the respondents are serving the hotel industry at the age of 5 years and below, and 34 percent are over 5.1 years.

1.7. Hotel Classification Level. Forty-seven percent of the respondents are working in the 5-Star hotels, while 39 percent at the 4-Star hotels and 14 percent at the 3-Star hotels.

2. Respondents' Assessment in the Hotel Industry's Rank-and-file Employees through the Retention Management's Success Factors

2.1. On the level of influence, both respondents consider compensation and benefits, work environment and corporate culture, and communication as the top 3 priorities while performance management and evaluation, recognition and rewards, career development and training, job design and work teams, and recruitment and selection are the last five priorities.

2.2. On the level of importance both respondents rate communication, performance management, and work environment and corporate culture as top 3 priorities, while compensation and benefits, career development and training, job design, recruitment, and recognition and rewards are the last five priorities.

2.3. On the level of influence and importance, compensation and benefits, communication, and work environment and corporate culture, are the top 3 priorities while performance management and evaluation, career development and training, job design and work teams, recognition and rewards, recruitment and selection are the last five priorities.

3. Significant Relationship between the Demographic Profiles of the Respondents and the Influence and the Level of Importance of Retention Factors

3.1. The level of influence shows the age ($rxy=0.1845$), and p, at 0.0108; highest educational attainment ($rxy=0.2886$), and p, at 0.0000; hotel classification ($rxy=0.1941$), and p, at 0.0108; position ($rxy=0.1534$)

and p, at 0.0480; and years of service (rxy=0.2415) and p, at 0.0006. The computed coefficients of the five demographic profiles are higher compared to their tabular or critical value (two-tailed) distribution; therefore the hypothesis is rejected, a significant relationship between demographic profiles and level of influence of retention factors.

3.2. The level of importance on the retention factors shows the age (rxy=0.6712), and p, at 0.0000; highest educational attainment (rxy=0.3323), and p, at 0.0000; hotel classification (rxy=0.2093), and p, at 0.0045; position (rxy=0.1986) and p, at 0.0107; and years of service (rxy=0.1988) and p, at 0.0107. The variables are significantly related to the level of importance of retention factors because the computed correlation coefficients are higher compared to the critical or tabular values at significant levels not exceeding 0.05 in a 2-tailed distribution. Therefore, the hypothesis is rejected because there is a significant relationship between a profile and level of importance of retention factors.

3.3. Relationship Between Managers Profile and Retention Factors

(1) Marital Status and Level of Influence. The marital status (rxy=-0.3480) of managers is significantly related to the level of influence of retention factors. The negative correlation coefficient means that a high level of influence in one marital status suffices low level of influence with that of the others or vice versa. Since the computed correlation coefficient is greater than its tabular or critical value (rxy=-0.3480 > p, 0.0194), the hypothesis is rejected because marital status is significantly related to the level of influence of retention factors.

(2) Age Profile and Level of Importance. The age (rxy=0.6776) is significantly related to the perceived level of importance of retention factors by managers. With the computed coefficient higher than its tabular or critical value (rxy=0.6776 > p, 0.0000), the hypothesis is rejected. The result shows that the relationship between age of managers and their assessment on the level of importance of retention factors was significant.

3.4. Relationship Between Rank-and-File Profile and Retention Factors

(1) Rank-and-File Profiles and Level of Influence. The highest educational attainment (rxy=0.2822) with p, at 0.0000 and hotel classification (rxy=0.2197) with p, at 0.0045 are significantly related to the level of influence of retention factors. The data shows that they are greater than their tabular or critical values in a 2-tailed distribution table. Thus, the hypothesis is rejected because the highest educational attainment and hotel classification are significantly related to the level of influence of retention factors.

(2) Rank-and-File Profiles and Level of Importance. The gender profile (rxy=0.1697), with a p at 0.0236; highest educational attainment (rxy=0.2707), with a p at 0.0002, hotel classification (rxy=0.2363) with a p at 0.0015; and years of service (rxy=-0.1339) with a p at 0.0485 are significantly related to the level of importance of retention factors and to be greater than their tabular or critical value in a 2-tailed distribution. Therefore, the hypothesis is rejected. A significant relationship exists between a profile (gender, highest educational attainment, hotel classification and years of service) and level of importance of retention factors as perceived by rank-and-file employees.

4. Significant Differences between the Respondents' Assessments on the Influence and Importance of Retention Factors

4.1. The significant difference in the level of influence of retention factors using a first assumption of two sample sizes have equal variances, the computed value of t is 2.01. It is revealed that t-computed is greater than t-tabular based on the value found at 248 degrees of freedom (t=2.01> p, 0.045514). The hypothesis is rejected because there is a significant difference between the perception of the managers and rank-and-file employees on the level of influence of retention factors.

The same is true on the second assumption that the two sample sizes have different variances, where the computed t (1.95) is greater than its tabular value at 66.75 degrees of freedom (t=1.95 > p, 0.027577). The hypothesis is likewise rejected because there is a significant difference between the perception of managers and rank-and-file employees on the level of influence of retention factors.

4.2. On the level of importance of retention factors using a first assumption that the two sample sizes have equal variances, the computed t (1.89) is greater than its tabular value at 248 degrees of freedom (t=1.89 > p, 0.029962). The hypothesis is rejected because there is a significant difference between the assessment of managers and rank-and-file employees on the level of importance of retention factors.

On the second assumption that the two independent samples have unequal sample variances, the computed t value is greater than its tabular value at 69.59 degrees of freedom (t=1.90 > p, 0.0304675). It means that the hypothesis is rejected because there is a significant difference in the perceptions of the managers and rank-and-file employees on the level of importance of retention factors.

5. The Role of Managers in the Retention Management of the Rank-and-file Employees on the Level of Influence and the Level of Importance

5.1. On the level of influence. The work environment and corporate culture (3.74) is assessed by managers to be the most influential success factor. Performance management and evaluation (3.70) and job design and work teams (3.66) complete the three most influential factors. It means that the retention of rank-and-file may be based on these three retention factors with the highest mean rating such that managers consider the three factors as strong considerations in their decision-making on issues about rank-and-file retention.

5.2. On the level of importance. The communication variable (3.89) is assessed as the most important among all retention factors. The reason is due to good communication skill is expected in the hospitality industry. Miscommunications often end in undesirable effects. It may affect the business operation and may even prolong in several periods. The respondent managers also consider recruitment and selection (3.87) as potent retention factor for rank-and-file. Another important factor is performance management and evaluation (3.83). This factor reflects the overall performance of the employee using performance appraisal and key performance indicators.

CONCLUSIONS

Based on the summary of findings, the following conclusions are presented.

1. The respondents' demographic profiles show eighty-one percent are rank-and-file level while the managers at 19 percent for the position level. Eighty-three percent of the respondents are professionals while thirteen percent are undergraduates in which 77 percent are on the rank-and-file positions. Sixty-seven percent comprises the lower age from 18 to 39 years old, and 33 percent composes the 40 years and above. Fifty-nine percent are males, and 41 percent represents the female. Fifty-five percent are married employees while 45 percent are single and widowed. About 66 percent of the respondents are serving the hotel industry at the age of 5 years and below, and 34 percent are over 5.1 years. Forty-seven percent of the respondents are working in the 5-Star hotels, while 53 percent at the 4 and 3-Star hotels

2. The respondents' assessment in the hotel industry's rank-and-file employees through the retention management's success factors on the level of influence and level of importance indicate that compensation and benefits, communication, and work environment and corporate culture are the top 3 priorities. The performance management and evaluation, career development

and training, job design and work teams, recognition and rewards, recruitment and selection are the last five priorities.
3. The significant relationship between the demographic profiles of the respondents and the level of influence and the level of importance in a relationship with age, highest educational attainment, hotel classification, position, and years of service shows significantly, and the hypothesis was statistically rejected. The relationship between managers' profile and retention factors in terms of marital status and level of influence, age profile, and level of importance, shows significant, and the hypothesis was rejected. The relationship between the rank-and-file profile such as the highest educational attainment and hotel classification and the retention factors in terms of the level of influence and level of importance shows significance and the hypothesis is statistically rejected. For the rank-and-file level of importance against gender, highest educational attainment, hotel classification, and years of service the hypothesis was statistically rejected because the data shows significance.
4. The significant difference in the level of influence and the level of importance of retention factors using the two assumptions of two sample sizes having equal and different variances, the hypothesis was rejected because there is a significant difference between the perception of the managers and rank-and-file employees.
5. The role of managers in the retention management of the rank-and-file employees shows the level of influence regarding the work environment and corporate culture as the most influential success factor. Performance management and evaluation and

job design and work teams complete the three most influential factors.

On the level of importance, communication was assessed as the most important among all retention factors for the reason that good communication skill is expected in the hospitality industry. The respondent managers also consider recruitment and selection as potent retention factor for rank-and-file, followed by performance management and evaluation.

RECOMMENDATIONS

1. The demographic profiles in the hotel industry should be put in the balance depending on the hotel establishment's requirements on the number of rank-and-file against the manager positions. In this study, eighty-one percent are in rank-and-file level while the managers at 19 percent for the position level. For retention management, hotel management should ensure that more employees will continue to work for over five years to maintain loyalty among the employees.
2. The hotel management should enhance the three success factors assessed by the rank-and-file employees as the top priority in terms of the level of influence and level of importance on the compensation and benefits, communication, and work environment and corporate culture while putting more emphasis in providing the other five success factors.
3. The hotel management should maintain the relationship of the level of influence and the level of importance with the respondents' profiles in terms of age, highest educational attainment, hotel classification, position, and years of service basing from their significance and rejection of the hypothesis.
4. The relationship between the managers' profile and retention factors in terms of marital status and level of influence, age profile, and level of importance, should be maintained as it was significantly assessed with the rejection of the hypothesis.

5. As to the relationship between the rank-and-file profile such as the highest educational attainment and hotel classification and the retention factors in terms of the level of influence and level of importance should also be enhanced as the hypothesis was being rejected.
6. For the rank-and-file level of importance against gender, highest educational attainment, hotel classification, and years of service this also needs enhancement basing from the hypothesis rejection.
7. The significant difference in the level of influence and the level of importance of retention factors using the two assumptions of two sample sizes having equal and different variances should also be enhanced due to the hypothesis rejection.
8. The role of managers in the retention management of the rank-and-file employees shows the level of influence regarding the work environment and corporate culture, performance management and evaluation and job design and work teams that must be nurtured for the hotel's sustainability.
9. On the level of importance, communication was assessed as the most important among all retention factors because good communication skill is expected in the hospitality industry. The respondent managers also consider recruitment and selection as potent retention factor for rank-and-file, followed by performance management and evaluation.
10. It is highly recommended that another research study should be conducted by another researcher to further enhance the six success factors as assessed by the respondents and find out if there will be additional success factors necessary to test the level of influence and level of importance in the retention of employees in the hotel industry.

BIBLIOGRAPHY

A. Published Articles and Journals

Agostino, Deborah and Arnaboldi, Michela (2015)The New Public Management inhybrid settings: New challenges for performance measures, *InternationalReview of Public Administration*, **20**, 4, (353).

Aguenza, B. B., & Som, A. P. M. (2018). Motivational factors of employee retentionand engagement in organizations. *IJAME*.

Alvarez (2017). Impact of Customer Relationship Management on Customer Loyalty, Customer Retention and Customer Profitability for Hotelier Sector, Journal of Systemics, Cybernetics and Informatics. 2017;15(4):36-43. Published by International Institute of Informatics and Cybernetics.

Ambrosius, J. (2018). Strategic talent management in emerging markets and itsimpact on employee retention: Evidence from Brazilian MNCs. *ThunderbirdInternational Business Review*, *60*(1), 53-68.and the service performance of student interns: Industry perspective. Publisher: African Online Scientific Information Systems. South African Journal of Business Management. 2015;46(3):1-10 DOI 10.4102/ sajbm.v46i3.96

Anitha, J. (2016). Role of Organizational Culture and Employee Commitment in Employee Retention. *ASBM Journal of Management*, *9*(1).

Aruna, M., & Anitha, J. (2015). Employee retention enablers: Generation Y employees. *SCMS Journal of Indian Management, 12*(3), 94.

Bidisha Lahkar Das, Dr. Mukulesh Baruah (2013). Employee Retention: Review of Literature. IOSR Journal of Business and Management (IOSR-JBM) e-ISSN: 2278-487X, p ISSN: 2319-7668. Volume 14, Issue 2 (Nov. - Dec. 2013), PP 08-16www.iosrjournals.org www.iosrjournals.org.

BK, Punia-Vision (2004). Employee empowerment and retention strategies in diversecorporate culture: A prognostic study.

Blalock, Ann Bonar (1999). Evaluation Research and the Performance Management

Clarke, Laura Hurd and Korotchenko (2011). Aging and the Body: A Review.

Published by Can J Aging, PMC 2014 Jun 26. DOI: 10.1017/S0714980811000274.

Cohn, Kenneth H. MD, MBA, FACS. The Effectiveness of Teamwork Training onTeamwork Behaviors and Team Performance: A Systematic Review andMeta-Analysis of Controlled Interventions.

C-S. Lee, C-W. Chao, H-I. Chen (2015). The relationship between HRM practices

Customer Orientation of Employees in Travel Agencies as a Predisposition of Service Quality: Test of Cose Consequences Model. Published by

International Journal for Quality Research. 2018;12(4):851-868 DOI 10.18421/IJQR12.04-05.

Dalibor Redžić (2016). Management in Hospitality sand Tourism. ISSN: 2620-0279

Das, Bidisha Lahkar, Baruah, Mukulesh (2013). Employee Retention: A Review of Deery, M., & Jago, L. (2015). Revisiting talent management, work-life balance andretention strategies. *International Journal of Contemporary HospitalityManagement, 27*(3), 453-472.

Feldman, D. (2000). The Dilbert syndrome: How employee cynicism aboutineffective management is changing the nature of careers in organizations. American Behavioral Scientist, 43, 1286-1301

Fernando, A. G. N. K., & Sutha, J. (2019). Influence of Internal Corporate SocialResponsibility on Employee Retention with Special Reference to the Apparel Industry in Sri Lanka. In *Cases on Corporate Social Responsibility andContemporary Issues in Organizations* (pp. 329-345). IGI Global.

Folakemi Ohunakin, Anthonia Adeniji, Olumuyiwa Oludayo, Omotayo Osibanjo

Gayialis, G.S.P.;Papadopoulos, A.S.; Ponis, P. T.; Vassilakopoulouand Tatsiopoulos, I. P. (2016). Integrating Process Modeling and Simulation with Benchmarking using a Business Process Management System for Local Government, *International Journal of Computer Theory and Engineering*, **8**,6, (482).

Havolli, Y. Human Resources Management. Research Institute RINVEST, Pristine;2005. https://doi.org/10.1111/1467-9299.00257

Huckel Schneider, Carmen; Milat, Andrew J.; and Moore, Gabriel (2016). Barriersand facilitators to evaluation of health policies and programs: Policymakerand researcher perspectives, *Evaluation and Program Planning*, **58**, (208).

Johennesse, L. A. C., & Chou, T. K. (2017). Employee Perceptions of TalentManagement Effectiveness on Retention. *Global Business & ManagementResearch*, *9*(3).

Jon R. Katzenbach, Douglas K. Smith: The Wisdom of Teams: Creating theHigh Performance Organization. New York, NY, Harper Business, 1994journals.sagepub.com

Kambere, G. (2018). Influence of employee empowerment on employee retention at Diamond Trust Bank Kenya limited (doctoral dissertation, school of business,University of Nairobi).

Karolina Simat, Ivana Blešić Sanja Božić, Miša Avramović Milan Ivkov (2018).

Khandelwal, A., & Shekhawat, N. (2018). Role of Talent Retention in ReducingEmployee Turnover.

Koli, Z. & Llaci, (2005). Sh. Human Resources Management. University BookPublishing House, Tirana;

Li Li, Shen mei Yuan, Nan Jiang (2014). An Analysis of the Influencing Factors of

Literature, IOSR Journal of Business and Management (IOSR-JBM) e-ISSN: 2278-487X, p-ISSN: 2319-7668. Volume 14, Issue 2 (Nov. - Dec. 2013), PP 08-16

Lochhead, C., & Stephens, A. (2004). Employee Retention, Labour Turnover and Knowledge Transfer: Case Studies from Canadian Plastics Sector. CanadianLabour and Business Centre (Centre Syndical et patronal du Canada)

Maccoby,E.E.(1984). Socialization and developmental change. Child Development,55, 317-328. Google Scholar management model: Integrating internal and external marketing functions", Journal of Services Marketing, Vol. 2 Issue: 1, pp.31-38, Published by MCB UP Ltd. https://doi.org/10.1108/eb024714

Mariani, Laura and Tieghi, Marco (2016). Measuring effectively in healthcare: Fromthe governance of the system to the management of the organizations, andback, *International Journal of Healthcare Management*, (0).

Mariani, Laura; Tieghi, Marco; and Gigli, Sabrina (2016). The efficacy of performance management system in healthcare. A literature review and research perspectives, *MANAGEMENT CONTROL*, 3, (97). Modern' Local Government, Journal of Services Marketing, Vol. Issue, pp. Movement: From Estrangement to Useful Integration? Journal of Services Marketing, Vol. Issue: https://doi.org/10.1177/13563899922208887

O'Herron, P., & Simonsen, P. (1995). Career development gets a charge at Sears Credit. Personnel Journal, 74 (5), 103-106 Published: January 13, 2017.

Papa, A., Dezi, L., Gregori, G. L., Mueller, J., & Miglietta, N. (2018). Improving innovation performance through knowledge acquisition: the moderating role of employee retention and human resource management practices. *Journal of Knowledge Management*.

Purnamasari, Detty; Wulandari, Lily; Ahmad Muhammad Thantawi and I WayanSimri Wicaksana (2016). Concept Similarity Searching for Support QueryRewriting, *International Journal of Computer Theory and Engineering*, **8**,6, (490).

Qesku, A. (2005). Assessment of individual achievement at work, Training Instituteof Public Administration TIPA-ITAP, Tirana.

Reeves, Dory (2016). Planning, Is It For You?, Management Skills for EffectivePlanners, 10.1007/978-1-137-27701-5_2, (10-33).

Rena, A. & Setyadi D. (2014). The Influence of Organizational Culture, Working Environment and Educational Training on Motivation and Performance of Government Employees at West Kutai Regency East Kalimanatan. EuropeanJourval of Business Management, Vol.6, No. 30

Rojas, Patricio (2016). Performance Assessment in the Public Sector – The Issue of Interpretation Asymmetries and Some Behavioral Responses, Performance Measurement and Management Control: Contemporary Issues, 10.1108/S1479-351220160000031011, (353-386).

Rossi and Natalia Aversano, Francesca Manes (2015). Advancing performance measurement, *International Journal of Productivity and Performance Management*, **64**, 1, (76).

Sandra-Dinora, Graciela, Tejeida-Padilla, Ricardo, Orantes-Jimenez, Vazquez-

(2018). Perception of frontline employees towards career growth opportunities: implications on turnover intention Publisher: Vilnius Gediminas Technical University. Business:Theory and Practice. 2018;19:278-287 DOI 10.3846/btp.2018.28 (Print); 2620-0481 (Online) Publisher: University of Kragujevac, Faculty of Hotel Management and Tourism in Vrnjačka Banja

Sanderson, Ian (2002). Performance Management, Evaluation and Learning in

service failure and service recovery in the hotel industry. Published by AOSIS Acta Commercii. 2006;6(1):162-172 DOI 10.4102/ac.v6i1.106

Sharon Lippincott: Meetings: Do's, Don'ts, and Donuts. Pittsburgh, PA, Lighthouse Point Press, 1994

Sinha, C. & Sinha, R. (2012). Factors Affecting Employee Retention: A Comparative Analysis of two Organizations from Heavy Engineering Industry, EuropeanJournal of Business and Management, Vol. 4, No. 3

Smith, Neale; Mitton, Craig; Hall, William; Bryan, Stirling; Donaldson, Cam;Peacock, Stuart; Gibson, Jennifer L.; and Urquhart, Bonnie (2016). High performance in healthcare priority setting and resource allocation: Aliterature- and case study-based framework in the Canadian context, *SocialScience & Medicine,* **162**, (185).

Tanwar, K., & Prasad, A. (2016). Exploring the relationship between employerbranding and employee retention. *Global Business Review*, *17*(3_suppl),186S-206S.

Thomas, Kenneth W. (2000) Intrinsic Motivation at Work: Building Energy and Commitment. San Francisco, CA, Berrett-Koehler Publishers.

Vecchio, R. P. (1993). The impact of differences in subordinate and supervisor age on attitudes and performance. *Psychology and Aging*, *8*(1), 112.

Woods, Ronald; Artist, Sarah; and O'Connor, Geraldine (2016). Learning in Australian local government: A roadmap for improving education &training, *Commonwealth Journal of Local Governance*, 18, (108).

B. Unpublished Doctoral Dissertation

Dy, Regina C. (2015). A Retention Model for Managerial Employees in Selected Food and Beverage Manufacturing Companies in Greater Manila Area. Doctoral Dissertation, University of Santo Thomas, Manila.

Macasa, Gerardo P., Jr. (2018). Determinants of Core Competencies of Top Executives in Managing Philippine Schools Overseas (PSO's): A Guide to Stakeholders and School Owners, a Doctoral Dissertation, Philippine Christian University, Manila.

C. Internet and Website

http://www.managementstudyguide.com/employee-retention.htm

https://www.google.ae/search?q=retention+management+meaning&oq=retention+management+meaning&aqs=chrome..69i57j0j69i60l2j0l2.5992j0j7&sourceid=chrome&ie=UTF-8

http://appraisals.naukrihub.com/definiton-concept.html

http://www.managementstudyguide.com/employeeretention.htmhttps://doi.org/10.13/journal.pone.0169604

https://www.google.ae/search?q=retention+management+meaning&oq=retention+mnagement+meaning&aqs=chrome..69i57j0j69i60l2j0l2.5992j0j7&sourceid=cromeie=UTF-8

Cohn, Kenneth H. Better Communication for Better Care: Mastering PhysicianAdministrator Collaboration. Chicago, IL, Health Administration Press, 2005, www.ache.org/pubs/redesign/productcatalog.cfm?pc=WWW1-2038.

Cohn, Kenneth H. (2006) Collaborate for Success! Breakthrough Strategies forEngaging Physicians, Nurses, and Hospital Executives. Chicago, IL, Health Administration Press, www.ache.org/hap.cfm.

McNamara 2008, Performance Management-Basic Concepts. Issued on 27th Mayhttp://www.managementhelp.org/perf_mng/perf_mng.htm

Performance Appraisal Feedback (2007). Issued on 21st May 2008 (Retrieved fromhttp://appraisals.naukrihub.com/pa-feedback.html)

Process of Performance Appraisal 2007. Issued on 21st May 2008http://appraisals. naukrihub.com/process.html

Tourism and Private sector in Abu Dhabi, April 2016, Issue 02-31032016. Retrieved from http://www.abudhabichamber.ae/PublicationsEnglish/Doc-19-4-2016-113051.pdf

Travel & Tourism Competitiveness Index 2017 edition. Retrieved from http://reports.weforum.org/travel-and-tourism-competitiveness-report 2017/country -profiles/#economy=ARE

Walker, K. & Moore, K. (2011). Performance Management and Evaluation: What's

The Difference? Retrieved from https://www.childtrends.org/wp content/uploads /2013/06/2011-02PerformMgmt.pdf. 20 August 2018

Warren, Christopher (2016). Importance of Corporate Memory – How collaboration and succession planning are integral to building knowledge management capabilities. Retrieved from https://www.linkedin.com/pulse/importance-corporate-memory-how-collaboration-planning-warren. Retrieved on 10 August 2018

Yazinski, S. (2009). Strategies for retaining employees and minimizing turnover.

Retrieved from http://hr.blr.com/whitepapers.aspxid=80396. European Journal of Business and Management www.iiste.org ISSN 2222-1905 (Paper) ISSN 2222-2839 (Online) Vol 4, No.3, 2012 148

APPENDICES

Appendix A

Letter Request on Conduct of the Survey Questionnaire

Date: December 1, 2018

Dear Sir / Madam,

Greetings!

I am a PhD candidate conducting my doctoral dissertation in Business Management at the Philippine Christian University's Graduate Program in the Middle East based in Abu Dhabi, UAE. My dissertation topic is "THE HOTEL INDUSTRY'S RETENTION MANAGEMENT'S SUCCESS FACTORS OF SELECTED MAJOR HOTELS IN ABU DHABI, UAE". This research is being conducted for the purpose of assessing the success factors that the hotel establishments are currently doing for their retention management program.

I am distributing a survey questionnaire for you to fill up as part of my data analysis to come up with the resolutions to the queries on the success factors being applied by the hotel industry in Abu Dhabi.

Your support is highly appreciated. Please be assured that all data will be treated with strict confidentially. Any result of the research study will not be divulged to anybody but on the general information to public information.

I hope to receive your most favorable reply within a short period of time. Please feel free to contact me at 056 525 6510 or eileen03811@gmail.com. Looking forward to receiving your favorable reply.

Respectfully Yours,

(SGD) **EILEEN GUERRA**
Ph.D. Candidate

Noted by;
(SGD) **Dr. Ed Malagapo**, Ph.D.
Dean, PCU Graduate School ME

Appendix B

Survey Questionnaire

Date: _____

Thank you for your time in answering the questions below. Please check the appropriate box.

Part 1. Demographic Profiles

Position Level: ☐ Rank and File ☐ Manager	Highest Educational Attainment ☐ Undergraduate ☐ College Graduate ☐ Master's Degree ☐ Doctorate Degree	Age: ☐ 18 to 29 years old ☐ 30 to 39 years old ☐ 40 to 49 years old ☐ 50 to 59 years old ☐ 60 years old and above
Gender: ☐ Male ☐ Female	Marital Status: ☐ Single ☐ Married ☐ Single Parent ☐ Widow / Widower	Years in the Company: ☐ 2 years or less ☐ 2.1 years to 5 years ☐ 5.1 years to 8 years ☐ Over 8 years

Part II. Success Factors

Please check the appropriate box that best corresponds to your thoughts and feelings **about** your work. Rest assure that all responses will be treated with confidentiality. Kindly answer the questions honestly using the following as a guide:

Likert Scale Table

Scale	Statistical Range	Interpretation	Level
5	4.21 – 5.00	Very Satisfied (VS)	Very High
4	3.41 – 4.20	Satisfied (SA)	High
3	2.61 – 3.40	Average (AV)	Average
2	1.81 – 2.60	Dissatisfied (DI)	Low
1	1.00 – 1.80	Very Dissatisfied (VD)	Very Low

Level of influence – the capacity of the factor to influence my behavior and/or judgment in staying with the company.

Level of importance – the factor having great significance and/or value to me to stay with the company.

No.	Factors	Level of Influence	Level of Importance
1	Compensation and benefits		
2	Recognition and Rewards		

3	Work Environment and Corporate Culture		
4	Recruitment and Selection		
5	Career Development and Training		
6	Job Design and Work Teams		
7	Performance Management and Evaluation		
8	Communication		

ABOUT THE AUTHOR

Dr. Eileen L. Guerra - Papellero was raised in Manila Philippines, She graduated from De La Salle University – College of Saint Benilde as BS-HRIM Hotel Restaurant Institute Management and completed her Ph.D in Business Management, Transnational Education Graduate Program Middle East in Philippine Christian University.

Based in United Arab Emirates, She's an Overseas Filipino Worker a formerly hotelier in Customer Service and Corporate Sales. Presently a Director of Sales and Marketing in Sentro Space – Dubai UAE. Prior She's one of the nominees in "Hospitality Professional of the Year" for two consecutive years (2017 & 2018) by the Filipino Times Award in Dubai, United Arab Emirates and Awarded on 2014 as "Kabayan of the month" reflecting credit and honor on the Filipino Community in UAE. She was awarded as Best Agent Supplier from VAV.ES 2014 (Spain). Eileen was also featured in Illustrado Magazine's- FILIPINO PROGRESS AND DIVERSITY AT THE WORK PLACE in June–July 2015.

Motivated to Execute in completion of her study and Climbing to the corporate ladder, Dr. Eileen's perseverance to grow and exposed to the Cultured World Class Heroes led her to aspired quietly and humbly thru the guidance of Almighty God that resonates her continuous learning through various stages of Development.

CURRICULUM VITAE

Eileen L. Guerra-Papellero
Mobile No. +9710503574983
Email Address: eileen03811@gmail.com
https://www.linkedin.com/in/dr-eileen-guerra-57408652/

May 7th, 2019 – Present **Start-Up**
Sentro Space – Dubai UAE
Director of Sales & Marketing

October 12th, 2011 – April 2019 **Re-Opening**
City Seasons Hotels 4* – Abu Dhabi & Dubai UAE
Royal Rose – 5* Star
Cluster Asst. Director – Sales – **(Promoted)** *January 1st, 2018*
Asst. Director – Sales – **(Promoted)** *October 1st, 2015*
Senior Sales Manager – **(Promoted)** *April 1st, 2014*
Sales Manager – Corporate
- Responsible for Corporate Segment with added accountability to some Airline and FIT Travel Trade
- Collaboration with 6 Executive
- Cross Selling – Al Ain & Oman

- Conversion of New Account with RFP's bidding
- Part of Re Opening and Refurbished till date
- Emerging positive direct relationships with key clients and business contacts
- Scheduling & Meet priorities and targets

July 10th, 2007 – March 05th, 2010 **Pre-Opening Hotel Apartment**
Flora Park & Flora Creek Deluxe Hotel Apartments
Sales Executive - *July 10th, 2007*
Asst. Sales Manager - *May 1, 2008 (**Promoted**)*
Sales Manager – *March 1, 2009 – March 5, 2010 (**Promoted**)*

- Promote the Product and Services of Both properties especially for the Corporate Companies
- Targeting the Key corporate accounts that can provide a numerous room reservation which will lead to a High Revenue
- Direct selling from office to office or door to door, Telesales-cold calling, set up an appointment, identifying the prospect's needs and then make an effective sales presentation.
- Mentoring in Training within the Department as well in training session

June 2003-July 2007 **Pre-Opening Hotel**
Novotel Accor – World Trade Center Dubai
RECEPTIONIST – *June 2003*
Front office Supervisor - December 2005- July 2007 (***Promoted***)
Providing Guest Information concerning Hotel's Facilities and Outlets. Performing any Necessary guest-related enquiry courtesy and effectively, even beyond the daily routine
such as cash float handling, guest account inquiry, cash collection, credit card, special billing, Check in

Check out Standard Procedure.

Communication and Dealing with any Departments and Division concerning thru Hospitality Operation.

Listen & strive to Guest Demand, request, complain, compliment & suggestion.

Monitoring and processing all late arrivals that occurs some departure, reservation and welcoming all

our guest with a genuine service that makes them

Responsible with other Handover and duties that has been given by superior or by both supervisor.

Maintaining a good working relationships within your team/colleague and guest and to control daily shift

operation within hours of duty

Ensure and Follow up for Market Share Competitors, House Status, Communicate and participate in Night

Auditing, Responsible to daily cashiering within the department

To be aware and coordinate within FO Department, other establishment as well with Housekeeping or

anything that may occur concerning with the job.

Assisting in the Training within the Department as well in training session

Oct 2002- May 2003
Mercantile Care Plans-Inc. Philippines
Agency Manager

Introduce and Promote, up selling to the General Public the Educare and Pension care Plans.

Responsible in Payment of the Plan Holder that must be remitted.

Prospecting and Recruitment of Quality Personnel whose engage in the Marketing

March 2017-May 2019

Philippine Christian University – Graduate Program Middle East

Ph.D. in Business Management (Candidate)

June 2009 – September 2010 – Graduate

Philippine Christian University – Graduate Program Middle East

MBA (*Master in Business of Administration*)

1998- October 20,2001

DE LA SALLE UNIVERSITY- COLLEGE OF SAINT BENILDE

BS-Hotel Restaurant and Institution Management

www.ingramcontent.com/pod-product-compliance
Lightning Source LLC
Chambersburg PA
CBHW030757180526
45163CB00003B/1056